Dekota Gregory is a Cherokee Indian from Locust Grove, Oklahoma, who stands firm in his faith and belief of God's plan. In 2018, he graduated from Oklahoma State University, where he met and lost his best friend and roommate. But through the experience, Dekota ultimately met the love of his life. Dekota felt God called him to use his writing talent as a sports journalist to share the story God gave him.

For my Savior and my wife, without whom, this book wouldn't have been possible.

Dekota Gregory

THE STORY OF MY STORY

AUSTIN MACAULEY PUBLISHERS™

LONDON · CAMBRIDGE · NEW YORK · SHARJAH

Ordering Information
Quantity sales: Special discounts are available on quantity purchases by corporations, associations, and others. For details, contact the publisher at the address below.

Publisher's Cataloging-in-Publication data
Gregory, Dekota
The Story of My Story

ISBN 9781645755302 (Paperback)
ISBN 9781645755296 (Hardback)
ISBN 9781645755319 (ePub e-book)

Library of Congress Control Number: 2020923821

www.austinmacauley.com/us

First Published (2021)
Austin Macauley Publishers LLC
40 Wall Street, 33rd Floor, Suite 3302
New York, NY 10005
USA

mail-usa@austinmacauley.com
+1 (646) 5125767

The Lord gave me this incredible story to share and put even more amazing people in my life to make everything possible. This book would not be possible without my wife, Sara, who supported me through everything. She's the love of my life and the reason behind all of my accomplishments. My parents, siblings, grandparents, aunts, uncles, and younger cousins have been my biggest fans no matter what I do and gave me the confidence to achieve any dream I've always wanted to. Of the amazing people outside of my family, Brandon tops the list. Not even an entire book can describe how impactful you were in such a short time, how much I love you, and how much we all still miss you. Ms. Cavazos is like having a little bit of Brandon still on Earth, and I wouldn't have written this book without her blessing. I also couldn't have published this book without everyone at Austin Macauley, who had faith in me and my work. Lastly, for the children I'll someday raise, I know a book is forever, so I want this one to always be a reminder to pursue any dream you have, trust in God's plan for you, and know that all these people I mentioned, and many others, love you and will do anything for you.

Introduction

I'd still have a love story with the same girl if what I'm about to tell you didn't happen. Or else I'd like to think so. When we told people how we met, it definitely wouldn't garner the same reactions it does today. But sometimes I do still tell people that we just met through a mutual friend. It's technically true, and much easier than going into detail.

Without this story, I could honestly tell people, "We met through a mutual friend," then whoever asked would slip a smile, and that part of the conversation would conclude. What I say now forces people to automatically react with, "Aww," then they slightly tilt their head and look at me as if I was just laid off.

Brandon would have eventually talked my wife into giving me a chance. He would have texted me throughout our first date and immediately after to see how it went. Even without what we had endured in our real scenario, I think my wife and I still would have clicked without suffering the lost we did. Brandon would have been thrilled.

Brandon would have been the one who eventually helped me pick out a ring to put on her finger and devise a plan for how to propose. He would have given me a pep talk before I asked for her father's blessing. He would have given me another speech on my wedding day, assuring me I was making the right decision before I handed him, my best man, the rings.

Brandon would have gotten a lecture himself, as well, from my bride-to-be, to protect the rings at all costs. It would be similar to the talk she gave him before my bachelor party, during which he promised, through an ornery grin, to keep me out of trouble and without a regrettable tattoo. The rest of my groomsmen would still be laughing at stories from the bachelor party as we helped each other get tuxes on in a tiny room with one body-length mirror, hangers, and athletic clothes scattered across the cement floor. Like he did before every job interview I had during college, Brandon would help me tie my tie as he repeated, "You got this, bud!"

But of the five men standing next to me on my wedding day, Brandon wasn't one of them.

No one texted and asked how our first date went. I was by myself when I bought the ring. I created a plan on my own. I encouraged myself before talking to my future father-in-law about having his daughter's hand in marriage. Someone else planned my bachelor party and had to listen to my bride's threats. It was a group effort before the wedding to calm my nerves.

As a Christian, I'm supposed to say Brandon was there with me on my wedding day, as well as every moment before and since. But Brandon wasn't really there, or else I could have seen him beaming or heard his laugh. Because on November 12th, 2016, Brandon, my best friend, my best man, never woke up.

I've told thousands of stories but never my own.

It's been my job since I was a junior at Locust Grove High School to share others' stories. I'm a sports journalist. It's the career I've dreamt about pursuing since I was in the fifth grade. All through elementary and middle school I kept my own stats and wrote stories about the games I watched on TV in a black one-subject notebook. As a high school junior, I got a part-time job with the local newspaper, traveling across Northeast Oklahoma to cover the Pirates, barely making enough to pay for the gas to drive my cherry red '02 Chevy Silverado everywhere I needed to be.

The dream of one day actually getting paid to watch sports and write was what consumed my life. It determined how I spent my free time, where I went to college, where I would eventually call home, knowing I had to escape my tiny hometown of only 1,300.

Writing other people's stories should have been my story. But apparently, my story is a love story. Or a tragedy. You can decide, I guess. It also has comedy, filled with mischief that only two college boys can get into. There are romantic gestures and a car wreck. There's even a puppy.

So maybe my story has everything to be a great tale. But despite that, I never thought to share my own story. I was taught as a sports writer to make athletes, these superhumans, look like normal people. And to make normal people look like those superhumans. I'm neither. I'm obviously not superhuman, and I don't think anyone has a normal story, so I've learned. But none of the writing I'm about to do was taught to me through experiences or while earning a bachelor's degree. Because, as I said, I've shared thousands of stories but never my own. None like this.

11

I also want to be real. I wouldn't write this unless I was being honest. At the church I attend, they preach, "Real people finding real hope, and experiencing real life in Christ." They put an emphasis on being real. That's why I share mistakes and experiences I'm not proud of. That's why I express emotions you may find strange. I can't expect you to trust my story if it's not even real.

So, here I am, starting to share my own story. I'm not in a press box, though. I'm writing from my best friend's bedroom. It's where I'm living right now, but I'm not rooming with him. Brandon died almost two years ago.

I'm living with Brandon's mom until I get married a month from now. Ms. Cavazos, like my mom, made sure I didn't move in with my fiancé before the wedding. Brandon's bedroom had been empty since his passing, and since he's pretty much the reason I'm about to get married and live in a different state now, he owed me a place to crash for a bit.

If you're not caught up yet, I'm writing from my best friend's bedroom who's no longer alive, but his death ultimately introduced me to my fiancé, so now I'm living in their hometown in Texas with Brandon's mom until the wedding. But it's really much more complex than that even.

This story is probably just as much about Brandon as it is about me. Without Brandon, there would probably be no story at all. But as much as I wish Brandon was also the end of this story, he's only the beginning.

Chapter 1

I'm honestly probably the most boring part of this story.

Like I mentioned, I'm an aspiring sports journalist. Of all the networking and handshaking I've done, I've never really met a truly interesting sports journalist. Most are white old men, usually raised in a middle-class family. That's me, I'm just not old, yet.

I'm Native American, like most folks in Oklahoma. I'm a member of the Cherokee Nation, but you probably couldn't tell by just looking at me because of my white skin and light-brown hair. My hair has even been close to blonde during some times of my life.

My looks can be deceiving, though, I guess. My appearance wouldn't hint that I've finished high school, nonetheless, I have a wife and a college degree.

I'm a Christian, dragged to church every Wednesday and Sunday, sometimes more, growing up with a mom and stepdad, who still lead the youth group at my home church. I'm not ashamed to say that's the most important part of who I am, and the biggest reason this story of mine was possible. God created this story; I'm just writing down what happened.

I'm probably describing every boy that grew up in small-town Oklahoma when talking about myself. My family is rooted in Locust Grove, Oklahoma, with all my grandparents, aunts, and uncles living within fifteen minutes of each other. Who I wasn't related to in the town might as well have been a relative because I either grew up with them or they were old enough to watch me grow up.

When I did leave Locust Grove, it was for college, at Oklahoma State University in Stillwater, about two hours from home. OSU is where I not only got my degree, but also where most of this story transpired. That's where my and Brandon's paths crossed, even though his background and upbringing was nothing like how I just described mine.

Brandon and I came from drastically different households. But looking back, our differences may have been what made our friendship work so well, somehow. And in some ways, it's even hard to spot a difference.

He couldn't believe towns like Locust Grove actually existed, where you walk into a restaurant to get pizza and know literally everyone in the building, from the owner who asked you how school was going, to the people in the next booth who asked if you were going to the game that night.

I was fascinated by the fact that Brandon lived only twenty minutes from AT&T Stadium, where the Dallas Cowboys play, and freshmen rarely made varsity teams at his high school. Coming from a town that had just built a Walmart, and only a neighborhood market at that, I couldn't comprehend that people could drive down the street to not only have a choice between Walmart and Target, but also have options of places to eat. Locust Grove has a Sonic,

Mazzio's, and three local restaurants, which will probably change by the time you're even reading this.

As for our family backgrounds, I grew up in two different households, spending most of my life under the same roof as my mom, stepdad, and a younger half-sister. My dad and I became pretty close while I was in high school, especially after I moved in with him later in high school. We still text each other about every day.

After plenty of nights sleeping on my dad's couch during visits with me, Brandon mentioned to me after almost every trip that he looked forward to being twenty-one so he could sit down and have a beer with my dad. That's a moment sons seem to look forward to have with their fathers for some reason, almost like becoming friends with your old man or something.

Brandon didn't really know his dad. It's crazy how God works, though. Brandon actually saw his dad the last time he was home before he died. Brandon's dad was temporarily working at the local Chili's and seated Brandon, who was with his aunts. Brandon had no clue who the man was, but his dad knew who Brandon was. He got the chance to see his son one last time before he never could again.

I obviously don't want to go into too much detail about all that because I don't want to overstep my boundaries with the Cavazos family, but I felt like that was an important anecdote to include. I mean, this 20-year-old young man died and made such an impact in that short time that there was standing room only at his funeral. All of those people raved about Brandon's smile and how incredible he was, but yet, his own father wouldn't actually know about any of that. But God still gave him one last look at Brandon, maybe even catching a glimpse of that smile he can now only hear descriptions of.

That way people talk about Brandon, that's also the way they think of Ms. Cavazos. She raised Brandon as a single mother with her cousin, Jamie, who lived with the family the whole time Ms. Cavazos raised her two sons, and still does today. Jamie became a needed co-parent, which honestly still astonishes me that she has enough love for Ms. Cavazos, Brandon, and his brother, Blaine, that she would move in and help raise them as her own.

Brandon was a huge example of who Ms. Cavazos and Jamie are. Although Brandon didn't have a dad, he didn't miss out on anything because of his mom and Jamie. He had a mother who was even a second mom to all his friends, especially to me, even as an adult, with my own mom now in a different state than me.

Brandon as a person makes more sense when you learn more about his family, like the fact he never met a stranger and made everyone feel like family. From not only his mom and Jamie, but to his grandma and aunts, they're all mirroring images of Brandon's personality.

The more people Brandon included with the family just meant more people for Ms. Cavazos to love. She still always tells me, and I've heard her say it to and about plenty of others, "Bubba loved you, so we love you."

Brandon was the first to accept me at OSU. Ms. Cavazos and Jamie were the second and third.

July 2, 2014, was when Brandon and I first met. When you can say this story basically starts.

Everyone but Brandon in that huddle seemed lost that day. We were high school graduates about to start our college journey at freshmen orientation but could barely form a circle when asked to. I was actually so lost that day I barely even made it there. I left in time to arrive at campus an hour early, but once I got there, the map on my phone had me driving laps around my new home. The OSU campus is covered in bricks, from every building to even roads, and after several laps, it was like even though I kept driving, I was seeing the same scenery.

I eventually made it to the correct parking garage on Duck Street, somehow. After parking, I had to find the right building while in a sprint. Once again, the brick buildings all looked the same. Some orange balloons eventually led me to a smiling face, who pointed me up a rounded staircase that led me to where I needed to be.

After signing in and taking a picture for my student I.D., I walked in the giant ballroom as the groups were being formed. While the middle of the room was filled with only college students grazing around like cattle, the outside walls were lined with tables, each representing a booth from a club or organization students could join. I was able to see and process only a few before another person wearing a bright orange polo asked me my intended major and told me where I could find my group.

I was still catching my breath when I walked into the group of peers either awkwardly staring down at their phone or others actually striking conversation with the person next to them. Brandon was probably one of the few creating small talk. I, on the other hand, immediately pulled my phone out of my pocket. It was the first chance I had to text

17

my family I made it safely. I also had no idea how to just start talking to a stranger. There were no strangers in Locust Grove, convincing me that I was pretty outgoing until I left such a familiar place.

I barely sent off my texts before we were instructed to gather in a circle. We were told our one common denominator for being in the group—all having a communication-related major—before being forced to already open up. It's crazy how saying your name, major, and where you're from can seem so agonizing. And it never gets easier for anyone, even though stating your name, class, and probably a random fact about you is a first-day tradition from grade school through college. My go-to in college was to tell people I was a Taylor Swift fanatic, with all of her CDs in the console of my truck. I figured that wasn't expected from the guy wearing a baseball cap, athletic shorts, and a T-shirt on the first day. I also thought, maybe, there was a girl in there who would see a sweet, sensitive side in me and make a point to talk to me after class.

But those introductions only ever got one person to approach me: Brandon. While most students in our circle stated their desired majors as strategic communications, marketing, or another degree you can actually get a job in, Brandon and I were the only ones who said sports media.

Brandon immediately approached me after the huddle broke, and we followed our leader to the next destination. He pointed out how he was surprised we were the only sports media majors in the group, considering OSU was one of only a few colleges in the country with such a program at the time.

Although we were hoping to pursue the same major, it was quickly obvious that Brandon and I probably had little in common. I was a tall and scrawny white kid, which I still am today. I blend in with just about every group I'm part of. I'll go to restaurants in other states and people will swear I look familiar until I convince them I'm just a common-looking dude.

Brandon, on the other hand, always stood out. The first thing I noticed about Brandon, physically, was his size. He lost a lot of weight in college, but even after that, he was still just big-boned. He wasn't a giant or anything, still a few inches shorter than me, but I was also about six-foot-two. He was just built like a guy who played on the offensive line for a Class 6A, Texas High School football team, which he did.

But if we're being honest, Brandon's size isn't why he was so noticeable in most groups he hung out with. It was honestly the color of his skin. Brandon was what he deemed "Blaxican," having a Mexican mother and an African-American father. It obviously gave him a dark complexion, and I heard many girls mention how pretty his skin was because of the combination.

Brandon's race or background never influenced who he hung out with, though. Most of his friends were white, never treating him any differently, but he still had plenty of friends from every race and ethnicity. Brandon always complained about how, if he ever did anything troublesome with friends growing up, he'd be the only one ever recognized and busted.

Brandon's hairstyle didn't help him blend in either, even though I never think camouflage was a goal of his. His curly black hair was cut as a Mohawk most of our time in college. That made his face pretty recognizable, along with the trimmed beard and diamond earrings.

Brandon and I both eventually worked for the O'Colly, OSU's student newspaper. As a sophomore, I was in the newspaper almost every edition, three times a week, with my name and headshot at the top of every article that year. Brandon, at this point writing only for fun, had a story make print only once. Only once was his name and picture printed in an O'Colly newspaper. But that day, standing in the Chick-Fil-A line, a girl recognized Brandon and asked if he wrote for the O'Colly. Brandon was not only recognized from his story, which I never was in four years, but also got the girl's number.

I couldn't believe it. He just said, "Dekota, I'm a Blaxican with a Mohawk and earrings, people remember me."

The only thing we seemed to have in common, the day we met, was the bummy-ness of our wardrobe, both wearing a T-shirt and athletic shorts for our first impression, except I was wearing an OSU baseball cap with the bill slightly bent since I didn't have a Mohawk to present to my new classmates.

Brandon introduced himself, forcing me to do the same. I was hounded with questions about myself from him, meant to be conversation starters, but I was too awkward to realize. The only time it seemed like Brandon wasn't trying to pry information out of me was when he was conversing with another student nearby.

Brandon never just chalked me up as rude or shy and continued to start conversations with me. He slowly peeled my layers back, not only that day, but for the rest of our friendship, like I was an onion, or Shrek.

I accepted that Brandon was going to be my buddy for the day, and I was happy about having a companion for such a big day. However, I really didn't see Brandon and me being friends after orientation concluded at the end of that day. But as he went on about his excitement to start college that August, Brandon raved about the fun we would have and the memories we would make.

I was more concerned about working at the O'Colly and gaining experience while earning my degree, having already emailed and kissed up to editors. Despite pursuing the same major as me, Brandon didn't even know what the O'Colly was. But still, he congratulated me on my plans to write for the paper and made it a big deal, even though all a student had to do was walk in the newsroom and an editor would assign them a story.

At this point, I kind of put my nose to the sky. I viewed college as a competition, and Brandon was just a challenger in my career field I knew I was ahead of at the time. I still kind of had that mindset throughout college, but, eventually, that didn't stop me from also helping my colleagues and "competitors."

Before college, I had never attended a real party in high school. Still naive, I had convinced myself I would finish college the same way. I planned to spend my weekends and free time working to gain experience or with my girlfriend at the time, because, yes, I took a girlfriend to college. When Brandon mentioned all the pretty girls around campus, I bragged about my relationship, not listening to the "Don't bring a relationship to college" advice.

You could say I was pretty straight-laced, I guess. Which, for most parents, seems like a dream, especially for a kid moving off to college. I wasn't perfect, though, far from it actually, still sinning like every other kid. But, for some reason, I thought college would be easier to start over as someone who did everything the right way. I was by no means a bad kid in high school, but in my mind, I would be "more adult" in college, thinking almost like my parents, choosing studying over socializing. As much as that seems like the ideal way to endure college, that mindset would have given me a dreadful college experience. Most of what I gained from college came away from the classroom and work.

Brandon eventually became the balance I didn't know I needed at the time. He kept me level both ways, also making sure I got my head on straight when I started to veer and get caught up with the wrong things. I did the same for him, which was a flawless plan until we both sometimes put the wrong things first or felt like it was okay to sleep in.

I learned that day, Brandon's mom wanted him to make the same right choices during our time away just like mine. My first moments with Ms. Cavazos was when my eyes started to open that, despite being so different from Brandon in many ways, we were also the same in enough to help us click. Even puzzle pieces are different, but what's the same is enough to keep two pieces together.

I'd say Brandon invited me to lunch with him and his family, but it was more like he politely told me I was going to eat with them. It's not like I had anyone else to sit with, anyway. I made the trip by myself since the drive wasn't that long for me. Ms. Cavazos and Jamie took the day off to make the trek and enjoy the experience with Brandon. Parents and guardians who attended had their own things to do while there, and lunch was when both groups met back up.

As we met back in the crowded room, still lined with the same tables but with wandering parents in the center instead of students, Ms. Cavazos found us before we found her.

The way she was darting toward us I thought Brandon was in trouble. I remember seeing her eyes widen when she saw Brandon, before a game face took over her expression, with her smile disappearing and her eyes shrinking as she exploded like a bucking bull out of a chute. Her hands were full of papers and brochures, piled on top of an already-filled bright orange plastic bag hanging from her arm. Jamie followed behind with even more brochures and free goodies, trying to keep up as Ms. Cavazos, with no available hands, used her hips to navigate around other parents meeting back up with their parents.

The look in her eyes, plus the only split second she stopped to give a dirty glance to a group that abruptly stopped in front her during her dash across the room, had me thinking to myself that this couldn't be a very friendly lady. She can't be anything like her son, who I've known for about two hours now.

She obviously had something to say to Brandon as soon as she reached us but was caught off-guard that I was still awkwardly standing next to her son with my hands clasped in front of me.

She smiled, "Who's your friend?"

Brandon said my name, referred to me as his "new friend," and told his mom I'd be joining them for lunch.

Ms. Cavazos just smiled again and said, "OK, great!" before introducing herself, then finally getting to what she hurried our way to discuss.

All of a sudden this woman, who I had just met, was treating me like her other son. Sentences that would have started with, "Brandon, you need to…" now began with, "You both need to…"

She threw some of the papers and brochures in Brandon's hands before dragging us from one booth to another, starting with every Christian-based organization or club.

Ms. Cavazos looked at me and Brandon sternly, "You'll need lots of Jesus time while you're here to stay out of trouble."

For future reference, neither of us took her advice, even if we should have.

We were like three pinballs flying across that room, with Jamie trying to quietly keep up. Ms. Cavazos questioned me about things I was interested in, then had me at a booth she remembered seeing before I could even finish my answer.

I know now that's not how Ms. Cavazos always is, acting as if she just chugged a five-hour energy and has mountains to move. However, I have seen her like that plenty of other times. It's just how she gets when she has a goal and is on a mission.

After we managed to swing by every booth in that room before lunchtime, the three of us scurried to the ballroom to eat. With lunch came a mellower Ms. Cavazos.

It was like I was still talking to Brandon as she fired the same questions at me that he did, along with motherly concerns I could barely answer.

Ms. Cavazos quickly learned where I was from, my plans to write for the O'Colly, why Brandon approached me, why my parents weren't there with me. Most of the information she gained came from Brandon. I was short-spoken, and Ms. Cavazos wanted details.

The rest of our meal was each telling the other what their day had consisted of so far, then mapping out their remaining time on campus and what to prepare for.

By the time we met back up with our peers, the group treated me and Brandon as if we were a pair that had been together our whole lives, rather than a few hours.

I was still on a waiting list for on-campus housing after signing up late because of scholarship issues. They joked how I was homeless or would be living in a closet first semester. Brandon, who I had known since that morning, responded that if it came to that I'd just crash with him for a little bit. Since he already had a roommate, Brandon mentioned we may have to share a bed. It was said in a more joking manner, but I also realized it wasn't a lie. Something made me believe that, even though we had just met, Brandon really would share part of his tiny dorm room with me if I needed a place to stay.

The day ended with a group picture I still can't find anywhere today. Then, after Brandon quickly followed me on all social media platforms and Ms. Cavazos forced a hug goodbye, I thought the friendship was over. I'd tell my family and friends about meeting Brandon because it'd ease their mind about me making new friends, but in reality, he'd probably become someone I'd recognize in a class a few semesters from now. This wasn't a book or a movie, I wouldn't actually find my best friend the first day I officially became an OSU student.

Chapter 2

Clifford was full, with barely enough room for me and a passenger.

Clifford was the name Brandon and I eventually gave my truck because of its cherry red paint. We based the name off "Clifford the Big Red Dog," a television show we both watched growing up. For some reason, Brandon had a thing for naming objects he used a lot. His silver Mustang was Leslie. His MacBook was MaCayla. His fan was Fantasia. Although the names never really served a purpose, they were usually pretty clever, and Brandon always made sure to use them since he took the time to think of a name.

Clifford was technically nameless at this point, but nonetheless, the single-cab truck had my belongings wherever we could fit them, from the truck bed, to behind the seats, to the passenger floorboard. My stepmom's SUV was packed, as well, hauling most of my stuff. All that could be seen through the back windshield were clothes on hangers piled on bags, suitcases, and a mini-fridge.

It was a group effort to load all my stuff the night before move-in day. I'm not at all a morning person, but for this occasion, I wanted to get on the road as the sun was just starting to peek over the top of the clouds. The only other time I was up this early was when my dad would drag me to the woods before sunrise to deer hunt almost every Saturday morning in November and December.

The excitement of move-in day never wore off for me or Brandon. For me, it was almost ceremonial. Not many people make it out of my tiny hometown, so the move-in day was the physical act of me leaving Locust Grove to go somewhere else where I could become more than I could in my hometown. I love my hometown and the people in it, however, because of its size, there are boundaries that can limit certain dreams. That perspective also tends to limit people's goals, leaving them to never really reach all they could be.

Three vehicles headed to Stillwater that morning. My girlfriend at the time joined me in Clifford, my dad and stepmom were in charge of the big load in the SUV, and my mom was even more help driving down in her Tahoe.

I was moving in the first day we could. It was the Monday of OSU's "Welcome Week," which the university hosted the week before classes started to help freshmen and newcomers get accustomed to the campus and meet new people. It was also just an excuse for sophomores, juniors, and seniors to migrate back a week early to party. Welcome Week was like college without the classes, which I guess is the real college experience for some.

Oh, and I did get a room, by the way. As one of the first few things to fall into place to make this story possible, I was placed in the same building as Brandon, only two floors above him in Wentz Hall. That proximity was probably the biggest piece of kindling for the ignition of my and Brandon's friendship.

Because of Ms. Cavazos's schedule, Brandon was moving in the day after me. We had messaged each other off and on since orientation, mainly discussing our move-in plans and roommates.

Brandon was excited about actually meeting his roommate, not just messaging him through Twitter. He ended up being nothing like either of us were expecting, but still became a major character in this story, even after Brandon's death.

I, on the other hand, was nervous about my living situation. I took Brandon's advice and found my roommate, Jason, on Twitter so we could get in touch before move-in day. I learned he had already been living there all summer because of summer classes, and he really didn't have much in our room, just his clothes and essentials.

During our short back-and-forth, Jason also casually mentioned something about jail time. He followed up by pretty much saying he was straightening up and trying to get back on track so he didn't squander his college opportunity. Still terrible at communicating, I didn't ask why he went to jail, or when, or for how long. I mentioned it to my girlfriend, but other than that, I wanted to pretend like it wasn't a thing. Like it was something I thought I heard but really hadn't, even though it was in writing.

My parents eventually found out, and my mom just saw it as an opportunity to be a Christian witness because he was obviously in a tough stage in life. My mom was probably right. Unfortunately, at that point in my life, I was rather useless when it came to achieving God's work. You'll soon realize that.

It's something easy to blame college for, but in reality, that time was probably the best opportunity I'll ever have to be an impactful Christian witness. That, and especially never building a relationship with Jason, are two of the biggest regrets I have from college.

After living with Jason for a year, pretty much sharing our own prison cell, I never even found out why my roommate spent time behind bars. I imagine drugs from the few stories he shared with me. But after we moved out Jason was only someone I waved at when we saw each other on campus.

Jason was quiet, though, even more so than me. I'm very outgoing once I get comfortable around you and know you're comfortable with me, but I never got that vibe from Jason.

Even when Jason spoke it was quiet, forcing you to actually put forth effort to even hear what he was saying. He talked smoothly, with what seemed like a few seconds between every word because they left his mouth so slowly.

Nonetheless, Jason had apparently somehow made quite a few friends during his summer on campus. Granted, he did have a high school friend who was also on campus because he was a member of OSU's track and field team. That friend had a personality similar to Brandon's, sparking most of Jason's new friendships, much like Brandon did for me throughout college.

But even though reaching out to someone was out of Jason's comfort zone, he still invited me to tag along with him for the rest of my move-in day, knowing I didn't have many friends there yet.

Sydnie, who was literally at the hospital the day I was born, was also attending OSU and moved in the same day. We have been friends since my original birthday, with our moms being friends since high school. My mom and I walked across campus, not knowing how far away she lived, to see her that day, and see if she needed help moving in.

Syd had even more family than I did helping her. She also already had plans for the rest of the day and night. If there's anyone I know who makes as many friends as Brandon, it'd be Syd. Because of that, she had a plethora of friends before she even stepped on campus. Syd honestly probably would have let me join her, but I didn't want to invite myself and intrude.

So after my family and girlfriend headed back to Locust Grove, I was pretty much on my own, resulting in me following Jason around the rest of the day like a lost puppy. I didn't make any real friends that day. Jason invited me to a party that evening/night, but I declined the offer. I was still determined to never become part of the party scene and wasn't going to let that mindset slip day one. That left me in this tiny room alone by dinner time. I warmed up my leftovers from lunch with my mom, then started organizing my room, trying to make this place my new home.

The room had two twin-sized beds on parallel walls. There was pretty much an imaginary line drawn down the middle of everyone's room to symbolize your designated space. Each side had the beds, with a large wooden desk and chair on the adjacent wall, and separate closets on the wall across from the desks. My side of the room also had my black mini fridge with a microwave stacked on top of it at the foot of my bed.

31

In between the closets were drawers below a table connected to the wall, where we placed my TV and PlayStation. The desk chairs were never actually used to sit at the desk, but were always positioned in the center of the room, waiting for someone, or a pair, to plop down and play a videogame. I also used my chair as a table to eat on sometimes once my desk was covered with books and loose paper.

The layout was a challenge to mold to feel like home. It had all my stuff, clothes crammed in the closet, and pictures displayed on the lone shelf above my bed. It still wasn't home, though; no matter how hard I tried to make it homey that evening and night.

That first day was the only day I hated being away at college. It makes me wonder how dreadful my college experience would have been had I never met Brandon. I may not have even stuck around at OSU, even though it was exactly where I wanted (and needed) to be. But the next day, almost the minute Brandon arrived on campus, Wentz Hall felt like it was right where I was supposed to be. It was an assurance that Oklahoma State University was now home.

The Cavazos family was running behind. They got to Stillwater probably only a few minutes after Brandon said they would, but considering that was the only thing I was looking forward to that next day, it seemed like I had been sitting in my dorm room by myself for hours.

I slept in as late as possible, hoping that would make time go by quicker. For a college student, sleeping in can mean close to 1 p.m., if not later. I think I was too early in my college years to enter full hibernation then, though, but I'm sure I still neared noon. Brandon and his family left

Bedford, Texas, first thing that morning, a four-hour drive I would eventually endure plenty myself.

In reality, I didn't actually have to wait long, but I was just so tired of being on my own. It had been less than twenty-four hours since I had moved, but I had never been in this position before, always having at least a parent around if I needed company. Growing up, I practically lived with my childhood best friend, Braden, during the summer or any kind of break from school. That meant even during long periods away from school I still always had a friend at least nearby, considering he lived only a short bike ride away.

Jason was gone and had been since he left for that party the night before, but it's not like he was much company anyway. I finally decided to go get lunch. That involved figuring out where to find food on campus on my own, something I planned on trying to do when Brandon got there so we could explore together. No one enjoys sitting in any public place by themselves, anyway. I always feel like I look creepy or something when I'm somewhere by myself, just texting everyone back and rotating social media apps to scroll through on my phone.

After I ordered a sandwich from the first place I walked upon across the parking lot, I brought my lunch back to my room to eat. Then, about two bites in, my phone lit up beside me, flashing a text from Brandon saying he was there and what his room number was. I inhaled the sandwich and tried to casually hurry to the eighth floor, two floors below my room.

The door was swung wide open, hiding the "824" on the front it. The tiny dorm room the same size as mine was packed with people everywhere. The familiar faces alerted me when to stop as I wandered down the hallway. It was only Brandon, his brother, his roommate, and Ms. Cavazos, but still. Is this what it looked like the day before when I was moving in with my family? I'm not claustrophobic, but that room looked like it would make me that way, barely enough space to move, with bodies and boxes scattered everywhere.

Brandon had a pair of boxes stacked in his arms. He tried to peek over the cardboard to see me, and with only his eyes looking over, he said hello. Before I could respond to Brandon's greeting, Ms. Cavazos was already coming in for a hug with a big smile on her face.

"You know by now that we like to hug," she said.

Ms. Cavazos immediately introduced me to Brandon's brother, Blaine, who also had to poke his head around a stack of boxes to make eye contact with me and nod his head. If Brandon had not greeted me first, I probably wouldn't have been able to tell Brandon and Blaine apart, considering I had seen Brandon in-person only once before. If it wasn't for their completely different tastes in style, I probably still would have had trouble differentiating them after the introduction.

It was crazy, though. This was the second time I had actually been around these people, at least Brandon and Ms. Cavazos, and they were acting as if I'd been part of their lives since I was wearing diapers. In reality, I had spent about half a day with Brandon and an hour lunch with Ms. Cavazos. Brandon's roommate, who was sitting on his bed observing the chaos in his room, later told us he assumed Brandon and I had been friends since at least high school

34

after noticing how Brandon and his family treated me. How quickly Brandon and I clicked also influenced that belief.

Ms. Cavazos invited me to lunch with them, but I had to decline since I had just eaten. She then hugged me again before she left, of course. She mentioned how she couldn't wait to see what our college journey had in store for me and Brandon, and that we would have a great time. Then came a quick lecture about staying out of trouble, as if she was like a mother to me, which she eventually was.

Since a few moments had passed since the last goodbye hug, Ms. Cavazos gave me another. She even hugged Brandon's roommate, who she had just met, just like she did to me only a month and a half before then. After an awkward handshake goodbye with Blaine, where I went for the business style and he was going for the half handshake, half hug (you know the situation I'm talking about), the Cavazos family was off again until Brandon would return by himself.

It was a lot quieter when I later walked into 824. The door was open, unveiling Brandon sitting on his bed, stressfully examining the boxes covering the other half of his bed and his side of the room. His mom had hung most of his clothes up in the closet, and although she probably offered to organize the rest of her son's belongings, too, Brandon apparently declined and was now probably in regret.

Nate, his roommate, was sitting in a chair next to his bed on the far side of the room. When I walked in and Brandon greeted me, Nate only darted his eyes toward me for a split second.

I glanced at Brandon after noticing Nate's shy reaction. Brandon introduced us to try and ease the awkwardness. I said something along the lines of "What's up" or "Nice to meet you." Again, Nate just looked at me for a second, not even fully turning his body away from the TV propped on his desk to give me half a head nod.

This guy was supposed to be a lot cooler than me. At least the way Brandon described him, anyway. I was given details of a guy who was planning to walk on to the football team, already had girls lined up before he even got to campus, and was popping up on my Twitter timeline almost every day, even though I didn't even follow him yet.

With a cream soda sitting on the table near him, he was looking down at his phone with Twitter visible on the screen. I had yet to see Nate stand up, but I could already tell he was shorter than I was, which surprised me considering he was planning to try and play quarterback at the Division-I level. He was stocky, but still not the size of the guys I saw playing on Saturdays.

Brandon had asked Nate if he was still planning on trying to walk on, noticing that Nate was guzzling down soda with tryouts only a few weeks away. Nate was blunt, as usual, just saying, "Yup."

Brandon had the same thought I did about Nate's stature compared to the average college quarterback.

"At quarterback?"

Nate again simply answered, "Yup."

Brandon asked about what all he was doing to prepare, especially with tryouts creeping so close.

"You been working out a lot and stuff?"

"Not really."

Brandon and I made eye contact as I listened to their short conversation, still standing only a few steps inside the doorway. Even without speaking it was obvious we were both wondering the same kind of things, like, is this guy crazy?

Nate didn't make the football team, jolting his intramural basketball career at OSU. Basketball was actually Nate's best sport, a three-point specialist, but for some reason he thought he had a better chance to play college football over basketball. I think it had something to do with the roster size.

Nate made the worst first impression possible, to say the least. A terrible first impression that lasted most of that year, to be honest. Although my roommate was difficult to talk to, Brandon had the same problem along with many others throughout that first year.

Despite all the downs we both had with Nate as freshmen, and even after, he was always there, though. Always. He was also a Sports Media major and worked with us at the O'Colly. When Brandon and I moved to a different residence sophomore year, Nate lived in the same building, too.

Nate wasn't a stocker by no means. He was just loyal. Most of my and Brandon's mutual friends have certain traits that Brandon excelled at and remind me of him, whether he rubbed off on them or they were just present before. Nate was loyal, a lot like Brandon.

We taught Nate how to do laundry after he just stared at the washer machine before Brandon finally showed him how to spin the knob. We helped him come out of his shell, as much as Nate can, anyway. As someone without a license, we even tried to teach Nate how to drive in an empty parking lot.

When I say "we," I mean Brandon, with me and other friends along to help with various life lessons. Brandon's relationship with Nate, I think, is a great representation of who Brandon was. Brandon couldn't stand Nate at times, and even wanted to move out of the room at one point freshman year, but for some reason, he continued to push and tolerate Nate.

I'll also be the first one to tell you that we were extremely tough on Nate sometimes, especially Brandon. But as we tolerated Nate, he did the same with us. Despite questioning almost every move he made, Nate never shut us out.

Without realizing it, we saw what was deep down in one another. Because of that, Nate became one of my most reliable friends during college, being the only friend who was literally there day two to graduation day.

Through teaching Nate many things freshman year, he gave us one of our favorite stories to tell in college. It took place during that first rough year, and was probably the peak of freshman Nate. It's a tale Brandon shared probably hundreds of times. He obviously told it better than I ever could considering he was there for it all, but Nate couldn't live this down so someone had to keep the story alive.

I can relay the details pretty well after hearing Brandon's side about a million times. It never got old. Nate is probably the only one to hear this story more than me, and I'm sure it got old after the first time.

It started with a phone call. Nate went down with a knee injury playing basketball at the Colvin Center, OSU's student fitness facility. For Nate's sake, we'll say he was going up for a dunk, even though I never saw his feet leave the wood court as he shot his twelfth three-pointer of the game. Nonetheless, he came down and crashed to the floor. Nate swore he heard something pop in his knee as he tumbled on the court.

Brandon was Nate's first phone call to come to the rescue. Nate was sure he tore his ACL, and it eventually turned out he was right.

With Nate crippled, Brandon pretty much had to carry Nate through the Colvin Center with help from some of the staff. That included across the basketball courts, through workout equipment, around hustling college students, up a flight of steps and a long ramp, through two sets of glass doors, and across the street and parking lot. Brandon's Mustang was the end of that journey, forcing Brandon to get Nate down that low and crammed into the tiny spot.

Nate was obviously in pain, but by the time they got to the hospital, that was apparently the least of his concerns. After talking about his pain level, Nate asked Brandon what he thought the doctors would do for it. Brandon thought he gave Nate a reassuring answer: "Probably just give you some hydrocodone. It'll make you feel a lot better."

Brandon had suffered sports injuries before, and like most of us, he assumed numbing the pain would be Nate's greatest relief.

This is when I can only imagine the panicked look that Brandon saw on Nate's face. Brandon was the first to learn that, in the seventeen years of Nate's life, he had never swallowed a pill.

"Never?" Brandon questioned.

"Never."

We all found it unbelievable, considering Nate played basketball and football most of his life. Participating in some kind of sport year-around is sure to inflict some pain that needs some relief, at least once.

While Brandon was first telling me this story, later on, I swear we noticed at the same time the shelf on Nate's side of the room that he used as his medicine cabinet. It was packed, but filled with only children's pain reliever and cough syrup. No pills to be seen. He had avoided pills for seventeen years and counting now.

The doctor walked in, forcing Nate to face his fear. Brandon saw the same look again on Nate's face as the doctor held a pill in the palm of his hand. As Nate was frozen and unable to get words out, Brandon had to speak for his roommate.

"He's never swallowed a pill before."

Brandon had to utter the words without letting a smirk show through.

The doctor took the news graciously, turning into a coach determined to push Nate to be the pill popper he knew he could be.

"It's simple, just throw your head back and swallow."

The doctor tried to explain while demonstrating the motions.

After a short pep talk from the doctor and Brandon, Nate had his first go at the pill in the doctor's hand. Nate popped the pill in his mouth, quickly took a swig of water from the cup he was given, then threw his head back just like the doctor had shown him.

Nate leveled his head to nod that the pill didn't go down his throat. He tried again, performing the same ritual as the time before.

"Nuh, uh."

I'll be honest, I don't remember how many coaching sessions and glasses of water it took to get to this point, but the doctor eventually left the room. Brandon and Nate just sat quietly as Brandon wondered to himself where the doctor took off to. Each time Nate failed to swallow that pill, it became harder and harder for Brandon not to laugh from the corner of the room, standing a few feet behind the doctor.

The doctor swung the door open with a cup of applesauce in one of his hands. That was the moment Brandon lost control of his laughter and started to chuckle under his breath.

Like a parent does with their toddler, the doctor fed Nate a spoonful of applesauce, hoping it would go down with the pill already in Nate's mouth. The doctor tried this twice before reaching what seemed to be his limit.

The doctor shoved the applesauce in Nate's face and told him to spit the pill out in the cup. The pill fell from Nate's mouth into the applesauce container. The doctor stirred the pill into the applesauce that was left and got the biggest spoonful he could. He instructed Nate to open his mouth, and what was probably the last attempt no matter the outcome, the doctor put the spoonful of applesauce into Nate's mouth, with the pill buried somewhere underneath.

Nate gulped. The inside of his mouth was empty when he opened up wide enough to please a dentist. There was no sign of applesauce or the pill. Nate had done it, he swallowed the pill!

Nate was given a prescription that day. But during his intense pain shortly after the injury, not to mention surgery and rehab later on, Nate took only two pills from that container. Nate had won that battle, but the pills ultimately won the war.

Chapter 3

I actually didn't know Brandon's last name until almost three months into our friendship.

As my generation often does, we exchanged social media usernames to stay in contact, particularly Snapchat and Twitter. My username, for every social media platform, was simply just my first and last name together, which you can do when your parents spelled your first name wrong. I hated the spelling of my name growing up because it's not like anyone pronounced it any differently than "Dakota," even with the different letter after the D. My mom intended for people to put a little bit of an emphasis on the E so my name wasn't said like "Duh-kota." I didn't even take the time to pronounce it differently, though. It was annoying to tell everyone they were saying my name wrong just so they'd over-emphasize the E sound like there were four E's in a row or something. Apparently, my parents knew what they were doing, though, because I like the fact my name is spelled uniquely now since I'm pretty much known only by my byline at the top of newspaper articles, or on the cover of a book now.

But if your name isn't as unique as mine, you're forced to add numbers, maybe even a middle name or nickname, to your social media username. Or make it something that has nothing to do with your name at all, such as the mascot of your favorite team or alma mater.

I don't recall all of Brandon's usernames being the same, but at least for Snapchat and Twitter, which is all I had of his at the time, he deemed himself "LeBrandon James" in one way or another. As a sports fan, I immediately recognized the play on words referencing NBA star, LeBron James. I just assumed it was because his name already sounded so similar to the athlete's name.

I mean, adding "Le" in front of Brandon James didn't take too much of an imagination. But, little did I know, that's not at all where his username came from.

Brandon was competitive, fueling his obsession with playing basketball. He played for hours every summer day in high school at a park near his house in Bedford. That was only a small part of the self-given nickname, though. That was more of the story he told when parents or adults asked why he referred to himself as "LeBrandon James."

Brandon was rarely actually "LeBrandon James" during daylight hours. Another hobby Brandon spent many of his summer, and college, hours doing was partying. While everyone seems to have that one sin that can overtake them at times, this was Brandon's.

I wouldn't classify Brandon as a "partier," though. I don't think partying is particular what Brandon enjoyed. He saw it more as a chance to socialize and make new friends.

Brandon was usually the only person in a room, no matter how crowded, who was bold enough to start a new conversation about anything with anyone and make a new friend. He eventually broke through with me, but others are even harder to crack than me. However, alcohol has a knack for loosening almost anyone up.

The party scene was one of the few places where everyone else was almost at Brandon's level of friendliness. Brandon thrived in that environment, bouncing from one group to the next for an inside joke, or picking out the loner who seemed uncomfortable, and turning their night around for the better. I never left a party I attended with Brandon without a new friend or befriending a whole group of pals.

Brandon's competitiveness and desire to make new friends meshed at the beer pong table, the centerfold of every party. I'm not sure if it's a good or bad thing to be known for, but Brandon was the best pong player I ever saw in college. My partying days are over now so I guess I can say he's the best pong player I'll ever witness.

The pong table was Brandon's wheelhouse. It's almost like a stage. He got to be the center of attention, and Brandon never shied away from the spotlight. He also got to compete, while also making new friends every time a new pair stepped up to challenge his dominance.

Brandon would introduce himself, then, before he splashed a white ping-pong ball into every red solo cup in front of his challengers, his enemies would be his friends. Brandon notched a win and two new pals with every round of beer pong. Some losers would return, hoping for revenge, but for the most part, the competitors cycled through as Brandon's win tally and friend count grew. Whoever was lucky enough to be Brandon's partner that night, which was me a lot of times in college, just got to be along for the ride, riding Brandon's coattails to beer pong wins and new friends.

This transpired at almost every party Brandon attended, and eventually ended when either everyone there had already been beaten, or was just scared of the challenge. While most like to brag about "running the table" at the party they went to over the weekend, Brandon was shutting down tables.

It's a tradition for an O'Colly editor to host a party for the entire staff at the end of each semester. By our third semester attending these gatherings, the pong table was usually pretty quiet because our co-workers got tired of losing to me and Brandon.

I'll take this time to brag about the one time I was playing just as well as Brandon. After several conquests at our first O'Colly party ever, a pair of seniors called "Next," sure we were on a roll only because we were beating fellow, inexperienced freshmen. The seniors watched and waited as the cups across from us started to dwindle. I caught one of my shots before it bounced off the table to the ground, and, because of house rules, I got to try again as long as it was a trick shot. I tossed the ball from behind my back. Splash! Game over.

I looked over at one of the seniors with a smirk across my face. He just shook his head in disbelief as he and everyone else gathered around dispersed. With hours still left before the end of the party, the pong table was already dead.

The craziest shot I ever saw came from Brandon, though, of course. The party host continued to mouth from across the table as the game went back and forth. As a fifth-year senior, he thought there was no way a freshman could pull off the upset. With one cup left, he made the comment, "This is where you choke."

Brandon grinned as he darted his eyes toward me and his partner. I was just a spectator this night, as another mutual friend was Brandon's partner. Neither of us had any idea what Brandon had in mind. He closed his eyes, then put his left hand over his face, with now only his smirk still visible on his face. He lifted his right hand with the white pong ball resting between his thumb and two fingers. He flicked his wrist as the ball soared and started to drop toward the last remaining cup. I thought what everyone else had to be thinking: *No way.*

Splash! Game over.

Brandon's partner jumped on Brandon's back in excitement. I threw my arms up in joy. The challengers, across the table, stared down at the ball now floating around the red solo cup.

Even before these moments, Brandon had earned the alter-ego, "LeBrandon James." He rarely missed or lost, and was always clutch.

Before I witnessed the greatness myself, I was oblivious to this nickname, which really didn't last after our freshman year. Brandon and I occasionally messaged each other through social media the month and a half between orientation and move-in day. After we eventually exchanged numbers to text, I labeled him as "Brandon James" in my phone, thinking that was his real name at the time.

I knew I wasn't sure that was his last time but didn't want to ask. I couldn't remember his mom's name, or else that would have given me my answer. She most likely introduced herself as "Ms. Cavazos," but I had so much information thrown at me that day that I wouldn't know if she said "Ms. Cavazos" or "Ms. James."

I searched for a "Brandon James" on Facebook and Instagram, but since that obviously wasn't his name, I never found Brandon on those platforms until later on. I just thought the fact that it sounded like a pretty common name was the reason I couldn't find him with a simple search. That, and we didn't have any mutual friends at the time.

I finally learned my new best friend's name about a month into our time at OSU when my girlfriend at the time visited me in Stillwater for the first time, other than move-in day. By this time, Brandon and I were together nearly every day, truly becoming best friends pretty quickly. At this point I assumed it'd be weird to ask Brandon his last name, realizing it's something I should obviously know by now. I also figured I'd casually find out soon, which I did.

We were sitting in the Starbucks drive-thru, with my girlfriend driving her car, me in the passenger's seat, and Brandon sprawled out in the backseat. Despite being in the awkward position of third wheel, Brandon was doing most of the talking, as usual. He even sat in the middle of the backseat, leaned up so his head was centered between me and my girlfriend upfront. Brandon made a comment about hating Taco Bell, stating that as half Mexican he wasn't allowed to like such an imposter.

"You're Mexican?" my girlfriend questioned.

"Duh," Brandon responded.

"My last name is Cavazos, with a Z. That's the second half of me being 'Blaxican.'"

Ahh, Cavazos! I thought to myself as I quickly zoned out while the two furthered the conversation. It was a surname I needed to know even more than I thought I did at the time, as I would one day be included in the Cavazos family.

Even though I'm a journalist, I'm not one to question someone and pry details from them. I think it's because that's my job. When something is deemed work, you don't also want to do it in your free time, even if it is just asking someone questions to learn more about them. Because of that, my girlfriend got most things about Brandon out of him for me. She'd question while I just listened. She visited quite a bit that first semester so she and Brandon sometimes got into some pretty deep conversations I was just there to eavesdrop.

For some reason, I always wanted to marry my high school sweetheart. It seemed to happen a lot in a small town, and to be able to tell my kids that kind of love story seemed like a fairytale. I had two serious girlfriends in high school, and, spoiler alert, neither ultimately worked out. Those love stories couldn't compare to the one I now get to share with my kids one day, though.

As much as everyone wants every relationship to work out, I think my thought process behind wanting to end up with my high school sweetheart was less about the relationship and more about the plan I had for my life. I ultimately just wanted to avoid turmoil. Marrying someone I met at a young age seemed like the easiest option. That meant no more breakups and always having someone by your side through everything. That was ignorant of me at the time, though. Without going through and overcoming the lows I did, no matter how big or small they seem now, my life wouldn't be as much of a high as it is today.

Now, I know there will be plenty more obstacles in my future, some maybe even bigger than what I've already faced, but from the difficulties I've endured, I know there's a reason behind every wall I run into. Whether you believe in God's plan or not, you're going to have these experiences, these good and bad times. God is just who I rely on during both, especially the tough times.

The first difficult time I faced in college, the first low I encountered away from home, happened to be a breakup with my high school sweetheart, who I had been dating for almost two years. It now seems laughable that I took it as hard as I did, naïve enough to not trust in God's plan. It would have been a lot easier to overcome had I, one, not looked at the wrong things to get me through it, and, two, known what was ahead. I now know God always has something better in store, and although I still can't ever see what the future holds after a bad time, I at least know the turbulence is worth flying through to a worthy destination we can't see through a storm at the time.

As Brandon and I experienced nearly every first together in college, a breakup was included in our affairs. Only two weeks after my girlfriend and I broke up, Brandon's girlfriend also ended it with him. He had known the girl since high school, where they met in a church youth group. They had been dating for only a few months after they reconnected early in our first semester.

Now, our second semesters at OSU were both starting with breakups. Mine happened the Sunday before classes even started again. Brandon's came two weekends later, the same night he was trying to get me to get overcome mine.

I was feeling depressed, to say the least. Like I mentioned before, I was taking this breakup a lot harder than I should have been. I even drove two hours to Locust Grove the next day to try and win her back with some sweet, romantic speech I thought of during my drive there.

I lost my appetite, barely eating the next week and beyond. I couldn't sleep, tossing and turning, thinking what could have gone better in the relationship. I was playing Ed Sheeran's "Thinking Out Loud," on a loop. It was a song Brandon enjoyed but grew to hate after constantly hearing it blare through my headphones or playing every time he got into my truck.

Until the day Brandon died, he still screamed in anger when he heard, "When your legs don't work like they used to before," knowing it just meant the start of that song.

I think that song was Brandon's breaking point. He finally had it and made it a mission to end my funk. We both thought the wrong things would cure my depression, though. While I should have prayed and clung to the fact that I knew God had someone better lined up for me, Brandon and I thought this breakup should be handled like any college boy does: with more girls and alcohol.

It wasn't just Brandon, though. Everyone gave me the same advice to look for a girl just to get over my ex. They all pointed out how I came from a graduating class of 87 students, only half being girls, and now I was on a college campus with thousands of pretty college girls. In Locust Grove, you can only say, "There's more fish in the pond," but now there literally was a sea with more fish for me.

Brandon was ultimately trying to be a good friend. It was honestly a gesture a lot of friends wouldn't have made, hanging out with someone so negative for a night, trying to force them to have a good time. Even though our execution was wrong, it still created memories we could eventually laugh about and learn from.

Brandon had the night planned, getting a bottle of our go-to whiskey at the time. He strategically didn't want to hang out with very many people, mainly knowing that if there were more people I would more likely clam up and avoid socializing very much.

Our night started at his girlfriend's dorm with her and her roommate. I'm not sure why Brandon thought my cure would be to see him in a relationship, but I think he had to hit two birds with one stone since his girlfriend also wanted to hang out that night. We weren't there long, though. Brandon, a Blaxican from the suburbs, with the help of his girlfriend and her roommate, taught me, a white boy from a tiny town that country music is practically written about, how to two-step. I still don't know how to two-step despite their efforts, and I have no idea where or why Brandon learned how to.

Brandon eventually decided we should leave for phase two of the night. He threw his drawstring backpack over his shoulders, and I followed him out of the dorm and across the parking lot to our building. The journey started with me slipping on icy steps just outside the doorway, leaving me on my butt. Thanks to what I had consumed that night it was more funny than painful, slowing down our trek across the parking lot as we calmed our laughter. We eventually made it to our building, up the elevator to Brandon's floor so we could make a pit stop at his room. Brandon got what he needed, then we walked up two flights of stairs to the top floor where my room was.

We immediately sat on my bed. Brandon opened up his backpack to realize we had forgotten the bottle of whiskey at his girlfriend's room. No problem, though; Brandon would just take the short walk over and grab it real quick. His girlfriend said she was going to shower then go to bed, so Brandon should catch her before she went to sleep. It's not like it had been long, as the only detour was my wipeout.

Brandon left and I laid back to relax in my bed. For what seemed like only a few minutes, I scrolled through social media on my phone and wondered what else the night included.

Then Brandon called. He must be back and forgot his key to get into our building. I answered to hear Brandon's voice trembling, and for the first time, it sounded like Brandon didn't know what to say.

"I'm in the basement. Come down here. Just please meet me in the basement. I need you right now."

Each sentence was chopped into pieces by deep breaths and stutters.

The basement had become my and Brandon's go-to spot freshman year. Most went down there only to do laundry, making it a quiet area with couches, tables, chairs, and space to accomplish whatever we needed to. We used it to do homework together, as well as plan our weekly sports radio show we hosted together on OSU's student radio station. There were usually a few other stragglers being productive while their clothes were washing, but since it was a Friday night, Brandon was down there by himself when I showed up, sitting on the same couch we always planned the radio show.

Brandon was sitting on the edge of the couch with his face buried in his hands. Something was obviously wrong. Brandon's normal position was taking up most of the couch with his arm over the back and his legs up on the table or another chair he pulled up.

I didn't know what to say so I just sat beside him with my hands in my lap. A few seconds passed before he started telling me what was going on with his head still down. Another guy was at his girlfriend's room when Brandon showed up there.

Brandon said he just walked in, grabbed what he needed, and walked out without saying anything to either one of them. It took a lot to make Brandon angry, but when he finally got to that point, he had quite the temper. He kept looking down at the top of his hand and rubbing it, leading me to realize that his knuckles were bright red and a little swollen. Never wanting to hurt anyone, Brandon tended to hit objects to get frustration out. This time it was a metal street sign on his way over and a piece of metal on the wall that covered where a laundry chute used to be in our residence hall. That metal cover still had an indention of Brandon's fist the day we moved out of Wentz Hall.

Still trying to hold back tears from all the anger and sadness, Brandon joked about how dumb he was when his temper took over.

"I'm an idiot. Even a wall would have been better than choosing metal to punch."

I couldn't tell you what all was said, but Brandon and I had our first serious conversation that night, sharing our emotions. We told each other how dumb we felt feeling this way about a girl and getting so emotional, thinking guys weren't supposed to take breakups that hard. He felt especially pathetic considering he was technically dating this girl only a few months.

In only a way Brandon could, though, he said he didn't want to ruin a night that was supposed to get me back to being myself. But now the night was about the both of us turning things around. We left the basement only to stumble upon what we thought was a miracle at the time.

Both putting fake smiles on our faces, we tried to put together a plan for the rest of the night as we waited for the elevator. Brandon needed to swing by his room, then we'd meet up at my place.

The planning halted when the elevator doors slid open. No one was on board, which was strange for a Friday night when so many people were coming and going. All there was, with what appeared to be a light shining down on it and opera music playing in the background, was a bottle of our favorite whiskey.

We stared in awe so long that the elevator doors started to slide shut without us in yet. We stormed in, rushing to the corner where the bottle was. I pushed the buttons to our floors as Brandon picked it up and looked around, as if we were overlooking someone else in the tiny elevator. He quickly shoved the bottle in his backpack before the elevator made it to the next floor.

We stood quietly for a few floors, trying to ponder what had just happened, before Brandon finally broke the silence.

"We're really about to turn breakups into one of our best nights, aren't we?"

And we did. To be honest, I don't remember what the rest of that night consisted of, and I know it wasn't as incredible as we acted like it was. I'm pretty sure we just invited a few friends over to my dorm room to share our story about the magical bottle of whiskey.

Nonetheless, it was a story that defined our friendship in a way. It showed how we always made the most of everything, even if there were obvious mistakes made along the way.

I believe if you think about two things hard enough, such as that night and my friendship with Brandon, a correlation will start. Whether the relation between the two events was forced or not, the next loss I encountered was Brandon's death, a loss so much worse than a breakup. But like that night, the best somehow came from it.

Chapter 4

Garth Brooks is a pretty big deal around Stillwater. The country music legend attended OSU and has never been shy to plead where his allegiance stands when it comes to cheering for the Cowboys. He's also somewhat of an epitome of the university.

One of my favorite OSU experiences, which has become somewhat of a tradition for students, is how everyone at any place in Stillwater sings as a belting chorus any time Garth Brooks's "Friends in Low Places" blares through speakers. It doesn't really matter where the music starts playing or what's going on before it came on, especially on The Strip—home of late-night restaurants and most of the bars in Stillwater—everyone will immediately start singing the words no matter what, even in mid-conversation.

The best venue for this sing-along is Boone Pickens Stadium, where thousands of fans sing the song at the top of their lungs during football games. The bigger the game the louder the chorus, as it sometimes gives you goosebumps up your arm when everyone reaches a new notch to scream "Oooooasis!" in synch.

I think my favorite part of this tradition is the comradery, almost like a giant group of friends joining as one to sing a familiar tune. It's one of those moments where you feel like you belong wherever you are during that moment. I think it's because people have the biggest impact on making one another feel welcomed and like they belong. Even an uncomfortable situation can feel enjoyable because of the right person.

Think about it, our lives pretty much revolve around relationships, whether it's romantic, friendly, or even family and co-workers. No matter the surrounding, people look for someone else to make them feel comfortable. That's why Brandon was so beloved. He was always that one guy you could count on to make you feel like you belonged anywhere.

Brandon made me relate to Garth Brooks, making sure I had friends, even during low places in my life. This is something I came to realize after I lost my best friend. It was almost like Brandon prepared me for the situation, making sure I had reliable friends in a time of need and loneliness.

I stepped on campus knowing a handful of high school classmates who were also attending OSU, particularly Syd, who remains a close friend of mine.

Then I obviously had Brandon because he reached out that summer day at orientation.

Other than that, I was starting my college journey with only myself in Stillwater. And although I made tremendous friends while working at the O'Colly, I probably never would have connected with anyone outside of work if not for Brandon.

I've already mentioned Nate, who, despite all the ups and downs, was always there in college. That same day I met Nate, the first day Brandon and I were on campus together, Brandon introduced me to three more people who became part of my college experience. The first two were the girl he eventually dated and her roommate, who I was around countless hours freshman year.

Brandon drug me to a trivia night at Edmon Low Library as part of Welcome Week events so he could rekindle his relationship with his future girlfriend, and also introduce me to more people while getting me out of my dorm room. When we left the library after trivia was over, there was a girl hanging out at the steps of the library. I'm honestly not sure how the conversation started, but it's not unusual that one sparked considering how outgoing both Brandon and Jade are.

Living on the same floor as me, Jade continued to pop up everywhere we went early that semester, eventually becoming one of our closest friends during freshman year and beyond. Over two years later, Jade was the first friend that knocked on my door the day Brandon died. I remember opening the door and seeing a completely different Jade. Someone who was always loud and smiling, and would usually just barge through any door, just stood in my doorway as tears streamed down her cheeks until she finally wrapped her arms around me for a hug. As we cried on each other's shoulders, it was the start of realizing the people Brandon had brought together, and we were all now leaning on each other after losing our glue.

Jade's personality almost mirrored Brandon's, which meant she knew even more people that were eventually introduced to us, as well, including Gloria.

I never actually met Gloria freshman year, even though Brandon had started to become friends with her. The timing was always off somehow. Gloria was almost always with Jade when they'd stop by Brandon's room, but by the time I got there, there'd only be a funny note on Brandon's dry erase board left from Gloria. I'd always ask who wrote the comical note, and every time Brandon would tell me, Gloria, then try to convince me that I had met her before.

It wasn't until Brandon and I lived together sophomore year that I saw the face behind the humorous notes freshman year. As usual, it was Jade and Gloria, and they came over to play Guitar Hero, which Brandon and I had to hunt down a PlayStation 2 for before Brandon ordered the game online. Brandon was one of those guys that found a way to excel at so many random things, such as Guitar Hero and solving a Rubik's Cube. I think it was part of being the life of the party, even when there wasn't really even a party.

Most of our night was spent picking new songs at the most difficult level to see if Brandon could maintain a perfect score. Gloria stayed so late that she didn't want to walk through campus to her dorm by herself at night so she crashed on our couch. Apparently, the couch wasn't comfortable because when I woke up the next morning Gloria was sprawled out on a chair, with one leg over an arm of the chair and her arms stretched across the back.

From that moment on, Gloria was always around. She and Jade even ended up living with Syd for a year because they all knew each other through me and Brandon.

Gloria and I didn't really bond until after Brandon's death, but I would still consider her one of my best friends by the end of college. I think we both saw a little bit of Brandon in each other.

Also, when I say Jade seemed to always be around freshman year, I mean ALWAYS. The eighth floor of Wentz, which was all-male, became a tight-knit group freshman year. There was always something going on there with the guys from the floor, plus me and Jade. There were nights when the elevator lobby was filled with tables and chairs pulled from other rooms so we could all play a card game. There would be dozens gathered in one room to watch a movie or pass around controllers during a Super Smash Bros. tournament on the GameCube. I even remember bikes being raced around the hall one time.

A large portion of the eighth floor came from the same high school in Tulsa, which was ultimately the foundation of that floor becoming such great friends, as the rest of their neighbors just joined their group. Of those was KJ.

Of course, Brandon introduced me to KJ. Brandon noticed KJ eating by himself one day while we were waiting for our food at a nearby sandwich shop on campus so we joined him for dinner. Brandon had initially clicked with KJ for the same reason he did with me, as KJ was also a Sports Media major.

Like Gloria, KJ became one of my best friends in college, especially after losing Brandon. But KJ and I were even closer. We lived together during our last two years of college, and he was eventually a member of my wedding party. In a way, Brandon forced me and KJ to be friends and live together, ultimately planning to live with us, too, eventually, but it didn't take long for my and KJ's friendship to be by choice.

KJ's best friend, since even before high school, was Gustavo. But I didn't even meet Gustavo through KJ. Gustavo also lived on the eighth floor, so when Brandon learned Gustavo had the same class as us our second semester, the three of us walked there and sat together every day. Well, I guess I can't say it was the three of us every day. That astronomy class ended up being the worst class we ever took in college, so other than test day, the complete trio rarely attended class.

The next worst class I ever attended was Spanish. Without Gustavo's help, I probably would have failed. Between helping me with Spanish homework and working on my truck after I wrecked it, it became obvious to me that Gustavo had a heart of gold and was an incredible friend to have around.

From friends Brandon introduced me to, then to their friends, and to their friends, I could list the people in my life because of Brandon all day. There's also a handful of Brandon's friends from Texas, who even before I moved to their state, treated me like I had been part of their group since high school.

They never argued when Brandon added me to their fantasy football league, even if they wished they had vetoed Brandon's decision after I won the league my first season. Because of most of that group, which also includes his brother Blaine, I'm not without friends today in a completely new state. Some of them were at my house just a few days ago to squish on my couch and watch a UFC fight. The next day that same group was at Ms. Cavazos's house to celebrate Blaine's birthday and support him as he watched Tom Brady and the Patriots (his favorite team) narrowly beat the Chiefs to go to the Super Bowl (again).

Brandon's friend, Suk, also from the fantasy football league, happened to be one of my wife's closest friends, too. He ultimately ended up being the one that talked her into taking a chance on dating me after we first started talking. I didn't even meet Suk until Brandon's funeral. Before that, we had just talked a few times on FaceTime when Brandon called him. Today, Suk will come over to eat lunch with me even when my wife is gone. He's technically more of my friend than hers now, considering he only comes over when it involves eating with me or watching a sporting event.

There's even Brandon's Sigma Chi fraternity pledge class, and that entire house, really, that, even though I wasn't a member, treated me and my friends as if we were brothers as we grieved Brandon's loss with them.

Sigma Chi hosted a candlelight vigil in memory of Brandon in front of OSU's student union the week after Brandon's death. Even though the fraternity was in charge of everything, they still asked me and KJ to speak at the vigil. We met all the guys at the Sigma Chi house before the vigil, and they let us walk over with them as if we were part of the fraternity.

I never realized the people around me until I lost who I really thought was the only good friend I had in Stillwater. When Brandon died, it was like the scene from "Field of Dreams," as more and more friends kept coming out of a cornfield for support. Except instead of a cornfield they kept walking through our door. Our house was never empty the week after Brandon died, with friends constantly checking up on us and also looking for the same support they were giving us. Those close to Brandon feel like we have some sort of special bond, even today. Per Ms. Cavazos's request, Brandon's friends still meet every fall for a Friendsgiving in Texas, which is big enough that a whole room has to be rented out at a local restaurant.

Because of Brandon, we all have friends in low places. Even though Brandon's gone, we know we're still not alone, and never will be, because those who knew Brandon also learned that you should never let anyone else be alone or without a friend.

Chapter 5

I felt like such a nerd. I couldn't get back to school quick enough. I was even upset about having to move in a day later than I wanted.

A summer away from Stillwater and Brandon, consumed by my first internship with a nearby newspaper and coaching a little league baseball team, was finally coming to end. I never thought I'd be saying summer was *finally* coming to an end. But I wanted to be back so bad. Yes, I loved being with my family all the time, but for me, Stillwater was now home. After a year there, I had never felt like I belonged somewhere so much before. Locust Grove was home, too, but I was born there. I actually chose Stillwater.

Brandon and I had decided early freshman year we were going to live together as sophomores. Not only would we be living with our best friend, but we were also upgrading to a suite at Bennett Hall. That meant our own rooms with privacy, no sharing a community bathroom with fifty other dudes, and even having a living room with extra space for friends to come visit.

Brandon moved in the day before me, that Monday, which was the start of Welcome Week, and the first day we were allowed to move in. That was also my plan, but because of some reason I don't even remember, I had to wait until that Tuesday. I think it had something to do with needing my dad and his truck to come with me so I had room for everything. Brandon didn't bother waiting on his mom. He packed extra light so he could cram all his belongings in his two-door Mustang. He eventually brought the rest of his stuff during his next two visits home.

Brandon called me the moment he got on campus, pumping my excitement level, even more, to get back. I asked about our room, but Brandon had called me before he even got that far. He was still walking to the dorm from his car, panting while he talked because he had to park so far away on such a hot August day. That meant I got a FaceTime call about an hour later for a virtual tour of our new living space, even though I'd get to see it in person in less than twenty-four hours.

I was there the next day, and after I unloaded and we both had lunch with my dad, Dekota and Brandon were officially back together in Stillwater. That was the start of my sophomore year—the beginning of what I would refer to as our "peak college year." Do you know how they portray college on TV and movies? Brandon and I got pretty close to that experience as sophomores.

I've mentioned several times how I've done things I shouldn't, especially in college, and sophomore year was when I messed up the most. And I can't blame it on Brandon. To be honest, if it wasn't for him dragging me out of bed almost every weekday morning, that may have been the end to my college career.

My mom asked me almost every time I came home if I had found a church in Stillwater to attend yet. I usually used work as an excuse. Sunday was a travel day a lot of times during football season if OSU was playing on the road. Once wrestling season started, there was a dual almost every Sunday afternoon. Both of those excuses rarely actually interfered with a church service. Traveling on a Sunday during football season happened maybe three times. Most wrestling duals started at two in the afternoon, giving me enough time to make it after a church service that ended at noon. I was honestly just avoiding church. I knew I was caring about the wrong things and doing things I shouldn't, so it was just easier for me to ignore that than confront it and change.

Brandon had become a pro at balancing a social life with everything else. He could also stay up as late as he wanted and still easily get up on time for class. I had not. I had three main concerns: a social life, class, and work. I apparently had only two choices to really focus on, and I didn't pick class.

Before our third roommate even moved in two days after me, we already had the mini-fridge full of beer and had put two desks together in his room to make a beer pong table. Like I said, priorities were not inline. The Wednesday of that week was supposed to be my first day covering OSU football for the O'Colly, but I went so hard my first night back that I overslept and missed media availability entirely. I almost lost that gig, which rarely went to sophomores, before it even started. But I promise, I made up for it and contributed more time to the O'Colly than almost anyone, which didn't help my grade situation.

I traveled to or through fifteen states that first semester of sophomore year from covering football for the O'Colly. Most of those miles came from a drive, yes, a drive, not a flight, to West Virginia and back to Oklahoma. There literally wasn't a trip I would turn down. I always saw it as an opportunity I couldn't pass up. Even though my grades suffered a large part because of that, I still don't at all regret that thought process. However, I'd probably want a do-over had I not survived the lapse in academics.

I was still in that phase where I wanted to focus on only me, which I started after my breakup. That's why I was consumed by work so much. I was also working out at least once a day. Always being tall and scrawny, I had gone from 125 pounds to about 175 when I finally stopped working out midway through my junior year.

My sophomore year, and even a little bit before and after, was not only the farthest I've ever been from God, but also the farthest I've been from myself. It's complicated, though, because even though I said I was the farthest I've ever been from myself, I was also consumed by myself. Everything was about me, and I also thought I was a lot more than what I really was.

The closest I ever got to giving God the glory for any of the opportunities he had given me was what we can call "Pridefully humble," when you thank God in a social media post that mentions "I" much more than God just to show off what you did. All Christians are probably guilty of this, and I still sometimes am.

Philippians 2:7-8 helped me realize how important humility is for Christians because it shows you that Jesus is literally the son of the creator of the universe and can do whatever he wants, but yet, he became a man on Earth, during a time that was not easy, to be one of us and live like us, just to die for us. That verse, along with being told "No" for almost an entire year when trying to start my career after college, is what humbled me. That period made me realize I wasn't as great as I thought I was, especially on my own.

However, at this time, I was excelling in my career and in better physical shape than I had ever been. That obviously went to my head, and I gave myself all the credit for my success. I forgot to ever thank God, who blessed me with my talent and put me in the right place to make the most of it. Not to mention my parents and family, who had pushed me to get that far and made it possible for me to even try and achieve my dream. Nonetheless, I was the guy flexing in the mirror, taking lots of selfies, and bragging about all the cool stuff I was getting to do. Looking back, I don't even think I'd enjoy hanging out with myself, but for some reason, Brandon still did.

Brandon and I were already best friends before that year started, but by the end of sophomore year, we were literally like brothers. We pushed each other to be the best we could, praising one another when we found success, but also critiquing when we needed to. Brandon wasn't afraid to humble me. We even fought like brothers sometimes, but by the end of the day, one of us would apologize, and we were saying we loved each other before we decided where to go eat for dinner.

We did everything together. We ate almost every meal together. Both in a health kick, we worked out at the same time every day. When I took a weekend trip to Locust Grove to see family, Brandon was usually tagging along. We developed our Sunday tradition, which revolved around fantasy football. Brandon would come in my room just before noon to wake me up as he unplugged my TV and carried it to the living room. By the time I joined him, he'd be sprawled across the chair, facing our entertainment center that had a TV where it was supposed to and another on top, with a football game playing on both monitors. I'd plop on the couch, and we wouldn't leave our spots until halftime, when we'd rush to Little Caesars for pizza and cheese sticks. This was the routine every single Sunday of football season, even after sophomore year.

I eventually became busier with work. Brandon quit working at the O'Colly shortly into our sophomore campaign after he switched his major from Sports Media to Sports Management. Brandon also decided to join a fraternity and rush Sigma Chi, which took up a big chunk of his time. But even then, no longer working together and pursuing different objectives, Brandon and I always made time for each other, whether it was still meeting at the Colvin Center to work out, grabbing dinner together, or even sitting in the living room to catch each other up on what was going on in our lives.

I actually hated the fact that Brandon was joining a frat, just because I knew it meant sharing time with him. I know I sound like a crazy girlfriend or something, but Brandon was who pushed me, who made light of tough times, and who I shared everything with. It seemed like every day threw a new struggle at me, and without Brandon around, there was no way I could relax about the situation or figure out how to handle it.

As for Brandon, a Blaxican with a Mohawk and fake diamond earrings who always wore athletic clothes and hated to be bossed around, I really have no idea why he ever wanted to join a fraternity. I asked him "Why?" dozens of times, but I really never got much more than, "I just want to," or, later on, he talked about the connections it would help him make for his career.

I actually think it had something to do with a chip on his shoulder. Brandon was a minority raised by a single mother. The stereotypical frat member is white, from a wealthy, two-parent household. Brandon had the desire to join a frat since day one at OSU, but because of the stereotypes, he was always told he shouldn't, or couldn't. So he did.

Brandon never wavered from being himself, though. But he still had a knack for fitting in while also standing out. If that doesn't make sense, then that's because you've never met Brandon.

At the end of every school year, Stillwater hosts Calf Fry, a Red Dirt Country music festival, the weekend before finals start. People come from all over and even from different schools for the three-day event. OSU is still considered an agriculture college that has a cowboy as its mascot, so you can imagine that Calf Fry is a pretty big deal for most students. For most. Some don't fit into a sea of rednecks throwing Coors Light cans in the air and belting out lyrics about trucks and dirt roads. Shoot, I'm from a small Oklahoma town and have even lived on a dirt road before, and I barely even fit in there.

A lot of students borrow cowboy boots from a friend and go buy a cheap button-up to wear to the event so they can fit in with the environment at Calf Fry. I even bummed

71

a pair of boots the first year I went, making me realize I was probably the only Locust Grove citizen who didn't own a pair of boots. Even when I didn't wear boots the last two years I went, I still picked out jeans and a button-up that seemed "redneck enough."

Brandon never bothered, though. He wore jeans when we went our freshman year, but after that, I don't think he even put in that much effort. He wore what he would to anywhere else. He sported shorts while every other male wore blue jeans. It was usually warm, and the festival was outside, so Brandon wasn't going to be uncomfortable just to match everyone else.

He replaced cowboy boots with his usual, black Nike tennis shoes with black Nike tube socks, the ones with the swoosh at the top. His torso was covered with a T-shirt. He also still wore his flat bill hat backward. It was a snapback so the snaps rested at his hairline, just above the fake diamond earrings in his ears.

Brandon was never shunned, though. Despite being the only one not wearing jeans at an after-party, Brandon was still the most beloved person at any party, whether it was before, during, or after the concert. He would plug his phone into the speaker to DJ, and even if he changed the Red Dirt Country that was on a loop, no one complained. He would square dance in the street or in the back of pick-up trucks with girls wearing Daisy Duke jean shorts and cowboy boots. He even taught several of those girls, and even guys wearing cowboy hats, pretending to be country for a weekend, how to two-step. It was quite the sight to witness a black man dressed in a flat bill hat and fake diamond earrings teach another dude wearing a cowboy hat and boots how to two-step.

Brandon did the same thing when it came to being a member of Sigma Chi. He immediately fit right in, even becoming the unofficial ring leader of his pledge class. You could always pick out who was a fraternity member on campus. Their hair would be fixed, usually pushed up and combed to the side. They'd wear a fraternity shirt, which was usually an odd color, with bright shorts that ended just above the knee, white Nike tube socks, and either leather sandals or low-cut tennis shoes, usually Converse.

Brandon still wore an orange OSU T-shirt and athletic shorts. The most he ever did to his hair was quickly run a comb through the Mohawk in the morning. Jewelry was pretty frowned upon in fraternities, but still, I rarely saw Brandon without earrings in.

The way I witnessed Brandon somehow camouflage into every environment but also stick out amazed me. I admired Brandon so much, and still do, but how he was always himself, he was like a role model in that perspective.

I always did the best I could to fit in. I honestly don't think I've ever had a desire to actually stand out, except in seventh-grade football when I wore bright-red high socks every game while the rest of my team had on white or black ankle socks. At that time in my life, especially as a college sophomore, I had absolutely no idea who I really was. It definitely wasn't the self-centered person I was then, or at least I hoped not. Brandon knew that wasn't who I was, either. Even if I couldn't see I wasn't comfortable in my own skin, even with all the muscles, it was obvious for Brandon. He also knew who I could really be when I figured

73

myself out. Thankfully, Brandon did realize I wasn't myself at the time, or else I probably would have messed up my chances with my future wife.

She was pretty good friends with Brandon, and like me, went to Brandon about every situation to seek encouragement and advice. She still lived in Bedford, Texas, Brandon's hometown, so up until this conversation, I had no idea she even existed. Brandon swore he had told me about her before this, but I'm terrible with names, so I'll probably remember the story, but no chance I can recall a name.

She was having boy trouble, which was apparently a pretty common thing and why Brandon was telling me about this on our way back from working out at the Colvin. She had extremely high morals, which was usually the cause of her relationship troubles.

Brandon went on to tell me about how she worked at an after-school program because she wanted to be a teacher. He told me a lot more about her, but I was pretty much zoned out with only one concern: Is she pretty?

The answer was yes, and still is yes. My eyes lit up. My best friend knew a single pretty blonde with blue eyes (my type)? I pulled out my phone ready to get her number. What a wingman!

Brandon even told me that he had told her a lot about me and wanted to set us up eventually.

"Well, then, buddy, set us up!"

I was waiting to get her number, Snapchat, something. But Brandon refused. I didn't understand.

"She's pretty, and you want to set us up anyway, so why are you interfering with true love? Do you not think your best friend is good enough for this girl?"

"Sara Park is wife material," he told me.

"You would just mess up your chance right now."

Chapter 6

When Ms. Cavazos attended grief counseling after Brandon's death, the therapist told her that people tend to give those they lost an unrealistic persona, almost idolizing them like they don't have any flaws. This seems obvious once you think about it. We're not going to try and remember the bad times or qualities of someone we miss. We know no one is perfect, no matter how much we love them, but sometimes you hang onto the good so much that their time on earth seems like a fable, and they were the main character that never did any wrong. For some reason, I thought about this a lot after Ms. Cavazos explained it to me.

Brandon obviously wasn't perfect, which you've all realized by now. His mom even knew that. But it's like being in love, when your significant others' faults or bad habits somehow make you care about them even more. Those imperfections are what make them who they are. Brandon had quite the smart mouth, and Ms. Cavazos found herself even missing Brandon talking back to her. Ms. Cavazos admitted she was guilty of idolizing Brandon, and I wondered if I was, too.

It's hard to try and judge a guy you miss and is no longer around. I tried to think about lies I had convinced myself were true about Brandon that made him seem larger than life. But the more I thought and reminisced, Brandon really was larger than life.

I've repeated how incredible of a friend Brandon was, and still is somehow, but maybe I haven't provided enough stories for proof yet. Yeah, he reached out to me and became my first friend in college, and he was always there to listen to problems or give advice. But every friendship starts with at least one of them reaching out, and people share their struggles in any relationship.

Brandon standing in the fountain in front of Edmon Low Library was the epitome of not only Brandon, but an incredible friend and human. The moment became the legend of Brandon Cavazos, but at that time we didn't know there would ever be a legend of Brandon Cavazos, only Brandon himself. But he did it, and I witnessed it. I even took the picture.

I was crammed in a car with two other student journalists somewhere between Iowa and Stillwater when I turned twenty as a sophomore. It was another O'Colly trip, which I seemed to take almost every weekend that fall. Football season was winding down, but wrestling season was now officially underway so we were driving back from the first dual of the season, which was hosted at the University of Iowa's football stadium.

Those of us in the car were watching the clock on the dash of the car waiting for it to flash midnight, but my phone vibrated at 11:59 p.m. Brandon's name lit up when I looked down. He managed to tell me happy birthday even before

77

the guys in the car with me as he yelled as soon as the clocked ticked. He then asked how far away we were. We were still a few hours away so I made sure to repeat that he didn't need to worry about staying up until I got back.

I was taken back with how quiet the background was, figuring he'd be somewhere on a Saturday night. Brandon just said he didn't feel like doing much so he stayed in and had been playing Guitar Hero. That's exactly where Brandon was and what he was doing when I got home early the next morning.

Nate was there, too. Nate and I share the same birthday, November 15th, however, he's a year younger despite being in the same class. It became somewhat of a tradition in college that Nate and I spent at least part of the night before our birthday together. As part of the tradition, he had been in our dorm waiting on me with Brandon. They actually didn't have anything planned. It was like two kids waiting on their dad to get home from work. When I arrived, it was just another person to join in and play Guitar Hero or NCAA Football '14. I was appreciative they even waited on me that whole time. But once I had been home for a bit, Brandon realized how standard of a night it was becoming even though we were celebrating birthdays.

Brandon and I found enjoyment from exploring campus late at night that year. Sometimes you just need to escape your confined beige walls. This experience made OSU feel even more like home. The campus would be so quiet and empty, appearing more freeing without students dashing to class in every direction and middle-aged men trying to hand you pamphlets about political agendas. It was just the campus: the red brick surrounding you, the old buildings, the green planted trees, the dead construction sites.

We even made friends a few times doing this when we'd run into another group of friends doing the same. But this time it was only us three wandering around. It was a Saturday night so people tend to avoid campus on the weekend, and by this time it was also probably past three in the morning the next Sunday.

We once befriended another group when we found them wading in the base of the fountain. Almost every OSU student puts at least their toes in the fountain on Library Lawn at least once before they graduate. Brandon had started wading in the base of the fountain nearly every time we went out and explored after that first time with that group of random strangers.

The fountain in front of Edmon Low Library is sort of iconic at OSU. It's tradition to dye the water orange to signify the start of America's Greatest Homecoming Celebration. Visiting opponents have even dyed it themselves the night before games.

It has two bases, with the bottom being just a shallow pool of water surrounded by gray granite. The base is short enough for dogs passing by to stop for a sip of water, or even hop in to give their paws a break from the sweltering cement. Up the cement stairs is the second base, just like the other, but with a large bowl on a granite block with water gushing out in the middle of the shallow water.

The fountain is hard not to admire, no matter how many times you rush by it on your way to class. I don't think I ever passed by it without noticing someone trying to get a picture of the landmark on their phone. We were doing just that when Brandon got the idea that cemented his legacy as an OSU student. As we stood at the top, with the towering brick library behind us, we could see library lawn stretched behind the fountain, beautified with its garden and green grass. There were four large patches of grass where students played Frisbee, taught their dogs how to fetch, or rested against their backpack on the ground and read a book. Between the empty lots was a garden with brick pathways separating each flowerbed, which all centered around a circular monument that I was told holds a time capsule that'll be opened long after I'm gone. A short brick wall and sidewalk disconnected the fountain and library from the nearest two grass patches.

I had just noticed Brandon's grin stretch across his face before he was throwing his stuff in my arms. I wasn't thrown off when he started taking his black, Nike tennis shoes off, assuming he was going to wade in the fountain's base like usual. I was confused, though, as he emptied his pockets and stripped off his orange T-shirt to reveal a black tank top underneath. I wasn't sure what he had planned and asked, "Why?"

"It's my best friend's birthday. It's gotta be memorable somehow."

Brandon already had his left foot in the water before he responded to my questioning. By the time he had both feet in and was wading deeper toward the actual fountain, he yelled without even looking back to see my and Nate's puzzled looks.

"Take a picture!"

I sat his belongings on the cement at my feet and quickly dug my phone out of my pocket. I looked up when I heard

Brandon yelp about how cold the water was. He was already tensed up and standing in the bowl, staring down at the water shooting up right in front of him. The bowl is probably about chest height so I wasn't even sure how he got up there so fast. He was already almost in position for a picture before I could get my phone ready.

Brandon looked away from the water and glanced back at me and Nate to smile. He looked so accomplished, like he knew this moment was about to be famously known, even though there were only two of us to witness the feat. I got the camera on my phone finally ready.

Brandon turned back toward the gushing water and stepped right in. There he stood, posing in the fountain in front of Edmon Low Library in the heart of the Oklahoma State University campus at about 3 a.m. on a cold November morning. He looked toward the sky, mouth open as if he was about to howl at the moon, his hands balled in fists in front of him as he flexed. It looked like he was in the middle of the water as it sprouted around him.

I couldn't tell you how many seconds he was actually in the water, but long enough to get a picture and take in the moment. Although nearly every OSU student can say their feet have been in the fountain, Brandon might have been the first to do what he did. He was pretty much baptized in the fountain.

Brandon jumped down from the bowl, waded through the water, and scurried across the cement back to us and his stuff. It took until the end of the brick sidewalk a few hundred feet from the fountain for Brandon to finally admit it was "a little cold but still worth it." We walked back to our room. Brandon's shoes squishing with every step was the only noise we could hear on the empty campus. We didn't know it, but Brandon Cavazos had just made his legacy.

Even though he asked me to take a picture, Brandon was really just in it for the memory. I sent the picture to him right away, but he never really shared it because he was afraid he'd get in trouble. He just wanted to make sure I had some kind of memory from my twentieth birthday, the last one I got to spend with him.

The picture from that shenanigan flooded social media after Brandon's death, even without the story behind it. It was as if Brandon was the one who made the fountain famous, not a homecoming tradition or its beauty. The picture is even tattooed on Blaine's shoulder.

That's what legends are made of.

Chapter 7

I wish I didn't have to write this chapter. But without this chapter, I guess there would really be no book.

I can still hear the trembling voices I listened to that day, as each one tried to find the words to utter. I can still feel the constant vibration of my phone getting notifications in my pocket, as friends tried to find out what was going on. The vibration of my phone only continued once we did learn what happened.

I can still see everyone's faces, like portraits with glossy eyes and looks of defeat. I just stared at gaze after gaze, all mixed with the emotion of sorrow, confusion, and anger.

I woke up that Saturday morning, that November 12th, 2016, morning, but my best friend didn't. I got out of bed with just enough time to shower and get ready for work. As a junior now, it was my second season covering Cowboy football for the O'Colly so I didn't get to Boone Pickens Stadium quite as early as I did the year before. It was a 2:30 p.m. kickoff against Texas Tech so I made sure to sleep in but still get to my seat in the press box with plenty of time to get situated and eat the same free barbeque as I watched players warm up on the shiny green turf below me.

Nothing was different about the game. We expected a shootout between two high-powered offenses, both with quarterbacks now playing in the NFL. It was just that, tied 28-28 at halftime. There was so much action that I hadn't gotten a chance to check my phone, lying face down next to my laptop. That was normal, though. My eyes rarely left my laptop or the field when there was action.

Usually, by the time I got to my phone, I already had notifications from a group message between me, Brandon, and KJ, who I now lived with while Brandon stayed in the Sigma Chi fraternity house. The messages always consisted of Brandon griping about the team, relishing about a spectacular play, or creating plans for that night. Brandon was usually napping on our couch by the time I finished writing my article and got home from a game, resting up before whatever he had planned.

Brandon hadn't sparked a conversation in the group text yet, though. Even stranger than not hearing from Brandon yet, I had an Instagram message from a friend of his, who I had actually never met before since she lived in Texas. She gave me her number and asked me to call her. I apologized that I couldn't because I was in a quiet press box.

"I think something happened to Brandon," she responded.

There was another guy I knew through Brandon who messaged me on Twitter about the time I got her response.

"Dude, call me."

As my mind raced to the worst, I thought surely not and hoped Brandon was in jail. Before I could start thinking about what he could have done to end up behind bars, his brother, Blaine, messaged me to call him, too. That was the third person needing me to call them. This made it obvious that something was wrong, but I thought if I didn't call, then I would never know, meaning nothing really happened. But I knew I had to call Blaine. He was family so he was either concerned or had something important to talk about. I escaped to the stairway and walked up a story so I could be by myself when I called Blaine.

About the time I was in the elevator, going up to the press box of Boone Pickens Stadium earlier that day, two police officers knocked on Ms. Cavazos's door. They told her that her son was dead. She said it couldn't be. But when they described the Texas outline tattooed on his forearm, she knew it was her boy.

I dropped and sat on the steps. I looked down at the cement between my shoes. Speechless, Blaine had to ask if I was still there. I managed to get out "Yeah," but I'm really not sure I said much else to him. I wish I could have, maybe helped comfort him or pray with him, but my mind couldn't comprehend what I had just heard.

In denial, I called the other friend, thinking surely he would tell me there was a mix-up. I didn't hear right. But he told me the same thing. Brandon was gone.

I felt like I should cry but no tears rolled from my eyes. I stood up to go to my next destination but stopped because I really had no idea where to go next. I would say a million thoughts went through my head, but I honestly don't think I was able to think of any.

I was teleported into a dream, a nightmare. I was moving but felt like I was going nowhere. I had no real control of myself or the environment around me. I was searching for KJ but saw only blurs as I walked through crowds of people. They were all smiling and cheering as the game kicked off again, oblivious that a young man had just lost his life only a few miles away. I guess part of me thought the whole world would pause for a moment of silence or something. I didn't understand how things were still proceeding as normal. Even KJ's life was the same, but I was going to be the one to change it forever. If I could ever find him. Unless I just waited so he could enjoy the game and more of his day. But I couldn't let him find out any other way than from my mouth.

KJ wasn't in his usual seats. He hadn't gotten a ticket for this game so he was outside the stadium tailgating. Again, he was having fun, but I was about to ruin it. KJ wouldn't answer his phone. He never did, but I figured because of the situation, fate would influence him to pick up. Gustavo answered but was at work, not with KJ. He could tell something was wrong, and it was so hard not to tell him what had happened to his friend, but I felt like KJ needed to be the first I told. I also thought KJ should be the one to tell Gustavo since they were much closer than I was with Gustavo.

I called another one of KJ's friends. I had talked to him only once before, but he immediately sensed uneasiness in my voice.

"KJ, it's Dekota. I think something's wrong."

I met KJ right outside the stadium. I told him. Telling someone else that Brandon had died made it real. The nightmare had ended and quickly became reality. I had to tell more friends. Like KJ, none of them immediately responded because of shock. That was the worst part about being one of the first friends to know: I had to tell others. I wish I could have just pretended nothing was going on and let them find out another way.

I eventually had to make phone calls to my parents, who both wanted to immediately drive to Stillwater to comfort me. I convinced them to wait until the next morning.

I told them everything I knew, but all I knew then was that Brandon was dead. I never learned the details all at once, probably because I never actually asked. I just pieced together parts of that morning as I heard new details.

Brandon didn't wake up that morning. He liked to sleep in so it took a while for someone to realize his eyes were still closed when they should have been opened. Brandon lived with five others in a room in the fraternity house, but only one other was still in town that weekend. He moved rooms in the middle of the night because Brandon's snoring was keeping him up. I don't blame him for anything.

I don't know who found Brandon or tried to wake him first. Knowing he was a heavy sleeper, they shook hard enough and yelled loud enough to wake anyone. Another called 9-1-1, a call that was later released to media. I've still never listened to it, though.

Weeks later, an autopsy report revealed why Brandon's life ended. The news said he died from alcohol poisoning. This made sense because we all saw the picture of him with a giant bottle of whiskey the night before. This caused most of his friends to try and blame whoever was with him that night, however, no one really knew who Brandon hung out with his final hours.

I had asked Brandon to come to the OSU basketball game with me and Pud, but he declined the invite. He texted and asked if he could hang out at my house with guys from the fraternity before they went out, but he never stopped by after his plans suddenly changed.

I thought I could have changed his life's ending had I talked him into going to the game with us or tagged along with him later. We all beat ourselves up trying to blame others or forming ways we could have changed the outcome. Brandon was a grown man, though. He just made a mistake we hoped the world wouldn't remember him by.

Ms. Cavazos also got a copy of that autopsy report. She read every word over and over, researching every statement she didn't understand. Yes, Brandon made a mistake, and we're not at all making excuses for his fault. We hope his outcome will prevent someone else from doing the same. But there was more to the autopsy report, we eventually learned.

Brandon had a heart condition. He had an enlarged heart, and probably had his entire life. He nor his family ever knew, though, despite yearly sports physicals and many doctor visits. The amount of alcohol Brandon consumed that night would not have killed a person with a normal heart. The enlarged heart is ultimately what killed him, influenced by the alcohol.

Brandon Cavazos died from having too big of a heart.

Chapter 8

I smiled a lot the days between Brandon's death and funeral.

That's crazy to think about and even more insane to actually write. It makes me feel like some sort of sociopath sometimes. I had just suffered the biggest loss of my life and was enduring the toughest obstacle I ever have, but yet, I continually caught myself grinning.

The night after Brandon died, friends were constantly in and out of our house. I would hear a knock and open the door to reveal a pitiful face staring through me. Most of those expressions involved tears, and I would usually start crying again with them as they hugged me in the doorway.

Jade was the first to stand in my doorway. She looked lost, like she was just wandering the neighborhood and somehow ended up at my address. She wasn't crying when I opened the door, but I could tell she had been. She pretty much fell into me as she wrapped her arms around me, and we cried together. A girl that always had something to say, it was the first time I had seen Jade speechless. She just cried and stared.

Pud did the same thing when I answered the door. Everyone's reaction was pretty much the same but yet so different. Pud knew Brandon through me, and they had bonded pretty quick the few times they had hung out. Pud's emotions were angrier than Jade's, though. As a cop himself, Pud had been hounding the Stillwater and OSU police departments trying to learn more details about why Brandon was dead since we didn't know anything yet. He wanted to know who was responsible and why it happened. I think he was more broken about seeing me the way I was than anything. I've always been like a little brother to Pud.

Friends from the O'Colly weren't close to Brandon but still acquaintances. They came in groups throughout the night to check in and bring leftovers from tailgates that day. My co-workers continued to be an extra support system as I grieved.

As the night progressed, emotions were less intense as others entered our house. A group of girls from Locust Grove didn't stop by until late that night. They had bonded with Brandon the past two years and were honestly closer to him than I was to them despite knowing all of them most of my life. I assumed they came so late because they waited to get themselves together. They wanted to take care of me but knew they couldn't if they were also still broken.

By the time they got there, it was just me and Mittens, my and KJ's roommate. I had known Mittens my whole life, but we weren't friends until he started at OSU in my sophomore year. Like me, Brandon forced Mittens out of his shell immediately. Brandon even gave him the nickname, Mittens, which he was eventually known to all our friends.

Mittens didn't go to the football game that Saturday because he was on his way back from something back home. He was sitting on the couch watching the game when

I came home before the contest had ended. He was obviously confused by my early arrival, so he was the second person I told about Brandon's death.

We just sat there in silence and watched the rest of the game. I noticed that he opened his mouth wanting to say something a few times, but I guess it wasn't important enough, or he decided he didn't really feel like talking.

OSU won by one point, thanks to Texas Tech's missed point-after attempt in the final seconds. Neither of us even reacted when the ball went wide of the yellow uprights. We were both staring at the TV, but I'm not sure how much of the game we were really watching.

Mittens and I hadn't eaten or left the house since I returned from the football game so the group of girls forced us to go to Whataburger with them. Just like any Texan, Whataburger was Brandon's favorite place to eat, which is why we ended up there.

Brandon had a bad habit of stealing the orange tents with order numbers and collecting them because, apparently, it was a common thing to do where he came from. The numbers he had hoarded were taped across the top of the wall in our dorm's living room sophomore year. We left gaps so we could insert new numbers in order. The orange tents, a poster with OSU's wrestling schedule, and a bronze fantasy football trophy on the entertainment stand were our only decorations in the room.

Because of Brandon and others like him, Stillwater's Whataburger became strict about getting its tents back. We hadn't added a new number from that location in almost a year despite frequent attempts. My order number that night was fifty-four, Brandon's favorite number that he wore on his football jersey in high school. Everyone at the table knew the significance of that number and pointed out the coincidence.

The tent was still sitting on our table after the worker handed out our food and gathered everyone else's numbers. I slipped it in my hoodie pocket and the orange tent numbered fifty-four eventually hung up in our living room. It was like Brandon already showing me that I could have a good time because of him without him. That was the first time I smiled after my best friend's death.

A few days later, I was driving my truck through our neighborhood when I found myself grinning again. It wasn't any kind of significant moment. I don't even remember what day it was or where I was coming from. I just smiled uncontrollably with Chance The Rapper probably blaring through my speakers.

I was obviously devastated about losing my best friend. I had spent the first hours after his death thinking about the time I missed with him. I still get jealous today of Brandon's friends who got to call him a companion long before I did. Chase was friends with Brandon since kindergarten. Why couldn't I have grown up with Brandon by my side? I got less than three years.

There was also the future. College is created to prepare young adults for what's ahead. That includes placing the right people in your life for what the future holds. Brandon was my right-hand man for whatever the future held. We had graduation, birthdays, weddings, parenthood, even more college left to make the most of together.

That thinking was selfish of me, though. I knew Brandon was in Heaven despite his recent mistakes. I shouldn't wish him back on this earth. Those thoughts also forced me to feel sorry for myself.

That moment in my truck was the first time I was grateful for the time I did get with Brandon. I got to make memories with him and call him my best friend, but what if we never met? What if instead of feeling the way I did, I just felt a second of pity when I heard about a fellow student losing his life? I would take the former without hesitation because the experiences were worth it. That's when I smiled. And that's why I kept smiling.

Maintaining a smile was easier because of the support I was surrounded with. My parents drove the two hours to Stillwater the morning after Brandon's death to be with me. Even after they left, our house was still full of friends playing ping-pong in the garage and eating pizza that someone ordered for us.

My grandparents made the same trip two days later. While Brandon died November 12th, my twenty-first birthday was November 15th. It was a day Brandon and I had circled on our calendars because of the significance, and a reason why people felt even sorrier for me about the situation. My grandma, who I've always called Big Mama despite her tiny stature, cooked lasagna and baked a cookie cake to bring to me the day before my birthday. She and my grandpa didn't stay long, but she wanted to make sure I had the right food to celebrate.

We had friends over that night and gathered around the cookie cake Big Mama baked as I blew out candles before we all chowed. Despite what we had all been through, and were still enduring, those people still took time to celebrate me, late at night in the middle of the week, even with school and work looming early the next morning. It's crazy to think how close the group surrounding me became from that moment on.

Braden drove from Locust Grove with another friend to make sure he was with his childhood best friend, not only on my birthday, but in a time of need. He woke up early the next morning to drive back two hours and make it to work on time. Syd and I have always been close, but she really was like a sister during that time, constantly checking up on me and trying to make me feel better. Gloria was the same. Our bond was already growing, but after losing Brandon, she became just as close to me as Syd. KJ and Mittens were there for everything, considering they lived with me. And, of course, as tradition, Nate was present that night, too, to celebrate our birthday.

Nate was turning only twenty at midnight. Pretty much that entire group, besides Syd, and me at midnight, was still under twenty-one. We all still scattered at midnight and sprinted to The Strip, where you officially become twenty-one in Stillwater. Syd and I met some of my co-workers from the O'Colly while the rest of the group waited at a food joint on the street. We made it quick, bouncing from one bar to the next before we met back up with the rest of our friends. We all then went where Brandon would have dragged us anyway: the casino.

I was back in bed before the bars even closed on The Strip that night. That was mainly because I had an important interview for an internship the next day, on my birthday.

I decided I wanted to become a sportswriter in the fifth-grade, maybe even earlier. My dad got a Tulsa World every Saturday and Sunday, and when he was finished reading, he'd give me the sports section, where I dreamt of someday seeing my byline. I was interviewing for the third time for an internship with the Tulsa World's sports staff.

I had somehow landed an interview as a freshman, which is when Brandon first taught me how to tie a tie. I tried tying my own before the interview sophomore year, but to no prevail, Brandon had to quickly do so before running off to class. I had other interviews and banquets, as well, so Brandon eventually learned that he needed to stick around to tie my tie whenever I had to wear one. I apparently caught on eventually, because before this third Tulsa World interview, the first one without Brandon giving me a pep talk while his hands flipped my tie over and under, I tied my tie myself. However, someone did have to fix it when I got to the newsroom, where everyone else from the O'Colly was gathered, frantically printing out resumes and articles as they waited for their time to go into the conference room where interviews were conducted.

I wasn't nervous at all that third time. It could have been from experience. Or because I had so much going on my mind couldn't afford to stress about anything else. I imitated Brandon's "false confidence" persona, however, I think he actually just had that much confidence and nailed the interview. I got the internship, which I learned a little over a month later.

Because of the internship and everything else going on, I was bustling from one appointment to the next on my birthday. That's exactly how I wanted it though, because the more I had happening, the less time to think about everything else going on.

I went from the interview to class, to a group picture, to home to quickly change, to work, to an organization meeting with a local sports editor, then to production night to help make the next day's newspaper.

I didn't work much that night, though. The O'Colly had a tradition of ordering a cake the last Friday of every month to celebrate birthdays, but Bob, our advisor, and an incredible leader, felt the need to do more for me. I actually felt bad for all these people who felt the need to go the extra mile for me then, but I also still can't explain how much I appreciate it.

Bob had Chick-Fil-A catered for everyone, plus a cake. She even got ahold of Jimmie Tramel, a mentor of mine, and he made the trip to celebrate with us. Jimmie is semi-famous around Locust Grove. He's worked at the Tulsa World almost his entire career, most of which was spent on the sports staff before eventually transferring to the scene department. Because we came from the same place, and because Jimmie is the most genuine guy you'll ever meet, he took me under his wing when I was still in high school and has mentored me ever since. I obviously appreciated all the texts he answered when I had questions and the crappy stories he looked over for me, but I couldn't believe a guy, even as kind as he is, would make that trip just to eat Chick-Fil-A with a college newspaper staff on my birthday and to check up on me.

When I laid in bed, the night Brandon died, I was actually dreading my birthday. I was already so upset about the future events I would experience without Brandon, and here was a monumental one only three days later. I was also worried about who was going to tie my tie for my interview that day. And how would I even stay composed during my interview with everything going on?

But the day was still special because of incredible people. It was the start of me realizing how blessed I still am today with the ones that God has placed in my life, even after thinking he took away the only close friend I had. But a lot of those amazing people in my life came through Brandon, including my wife.

Chapter 9

Brandon Cavazos is impossible to forget. That statement is true for any loved one we've lost, but yet after someone's death, we still routinely try obscure things to remember them, as if we'd forget their existence.

The details slip and the memories fade, but I'll always remember Brandon as a person and friend. I eventually started a blog to not only vent but also help document my stories of Brandon before all the details vanished me. It led to some of Brandon's other friends and family also being forced to reminisce and recollect memories they didn't know they still had. That process makes you realize the specifics you might have forgotten. Those details were probably lost long before your loved one's death, though. We don't think to store away memories for the time when that person is nothing but those memories. You may eventually start taking mental notes of a dying parent or grandparent, but I never thought I would ever need to remember anything about my twenty-year-old friend. I always imagined Brandon as a person, never a memory.

We discussed how odd it still seemed to hear people talk about Brandon like he wasn't still here. We were leaving Brandon's funeral service and headed to the cemetery. The pallbearers were all piled into one truck for the short trip. Ms. Cavazos asking if I'd be one of Brandon's pallbearers is still one of the biggest honors of my life, but at the same time, it was one I never wanted. I always thought the first time I bonded with all of Brandon's closest friends in a group would be at his wedding, not his funeral.

I was Brandon's only college friend that served as a pallbearer, with the rest being childhood friends or buddies since at least high school. That meant everyone knew each other pretty well except for me. I never felt left out, though. I rode down to the Bedford area for the funeral with my roommates, KJ and Mittens, Nate, and Gustavo. We were all welcomed with an invite to a bonfire the night before with a handful of mutual friends. Actually, how welcomed I felt that weekend was almost overwhelming.

My mind was still trying to comprehend what I was going through, and why I even had to endure my best friend's funeral at twenty-one, so there was no chance I'd remember all the people who introduced themselves and hugged me that weekend, and especially the day of the funeral. I feel bad about feeling this way, but I was honestly getting a little annoyed by all the affection I was getting. I didn't even get a chance to breathe between hugs and awkward conversations, or someone giving me that same look of pity and saying how sorry they felt for me.

It was obviously a situation I already hated. I thought sticking with the friends I came with and already knew would help my comfort level a bit, but I was almost immediately pulled away from my group and didn't see the guys I came with, or others I actually knew, until we were eating at the reception afterward.

I just stared at Brandon the entire service as people talked on the stage behind him, overlooking him and the congregation. I listened to almost everything they had to say, and everyone who spoke at Brandon's funeral did a tremendous job, but I just couldn't focus away from my best friend lying in a casket in front of the stage.

Brandon was wearing a Baltimore Ravens' Justin Tucker jersey. Only Brandon would be buried in a kicker's jersey. He wanted that jersey so bad. It was on his Christmas list every year, but somehow, that was always the one thing Ms. Cavazos forgot to get him. Brandon eventually gave up on getting it gifted to him and bought it for himself during sophomore year. We got notifications texted to us when we got a package sent to the front desk of our residence hall. Brandon sprinted down before he even read the entire notification and was already wearing the jersey when he walked back into our room with a grin stretched across his face.

Chase, Brandon's childhood best friend, Truman, a member of Brandon's Sigma Chi pledge class, and Ms. Cavazos spoke behind the pulpit as I gazed at my best friend lying in his casket. Ms. Cavazos was incredibly strong, giving us words of encouragement about counting down the days until we see Brandon again. She said each day without him was just another day closer to seeing him again. Ms. Cavazos still has a countdown on her phone, numbering how many days closer she is to seeing her son again. We also got a lecture about the dangers of alcohol from her, as if seeing our friend in a casket wasn't enough of a warning. And apparently, it wasn't for some.

Russell Gregory preached, and I honestly don't remember a word of his sermon. Russell is the Young Adult's Minister at Cross City Church First Euless, where the funeral was held. That's also where my wife and I attended church after we got married, with Russell in charge of our age group. I was drawn to that church two years later because of Russell, but it actually had nothing to do with that day, really.

The funeral was held in the church's chapel, which is smaller than the worship center where we attended service every Sunday. I still walked by it every week, though, as images from that day flashed through my thoughts. I saw how much more full it was for Brandon's funeral than whatever service the space is hosting that Sunday. The chapel was standing-room-only, with bodies blanketing the back wall during Brandon's funeral.

Russell is the father of another one of Brandon's pallbearers. That was really my main connection to him later on. We share the same last name but aren't related. Our connection definitely wasn't his sermon since I was zoned out most of it, staring at Brandon and secretly hoping I would see him move, proving it was all fake. Russell gave a sermon great enough to save my future wife that day, though, as she accepted Christ as her Savior. I'm thankful at least one of us was listening to Russell then.

You'd think that would have been the day I met my wife. She was there for it all: the service, the cemetery, the reception. Of all the people I met that day, not one was the person who knows me the best today.

That was a big day for her, though. Not only did she become a Christian, but it was also the first time she actually

101

saw me, the man she had no idea she'd eventually marry. I've heard her tell the story a handful of times. I was rushing in and out of the building during the reception, trying to get newspapers for everyone inside. Brandon was on the cover of the O'Colly the Monday after his death, and I also had a column about our friendship in that issue, so I had countless requests to bring copies for everyone to have. I then had to go back to the parking lot for a change of clothes before we left so I would be more comfortable on the road.

My future wife was standing by the door as I rushed back and forth. She says I caught her eye and she told her friend, "That's Dekota," as she stared. It was like she already knew me from all that Brandon had told her, but yet that was the first time I actually seemed like a real person to her. I eventually headed back to Stillwater without us ever saying a word to each other.

I got back to Stillwater thinking the grieving process was over since the funeral had come and gone. It's still not over, though. I'll actually be grieving Brandon longer than I even knew him.

The end of the semester was nearing, and we were cramming that short time with things to remember Brandon and be together. KJ and I made sure to put up my Christmas tree and ended up never taking it down until we moved after graduation.

My mom bought me and Brandon a white Christmas tree sophomore year that she made orange OSU ornaments to decorate with. Brandon and I spent the night before the Bedlam football game decorating the tree after Brandon spent an hour fluffing its branches. My favorite video is from that night. We had OSU's fight song blaring as I topped the tree with an orange foam finger instead of a star. Brandon cheered and chuckled as he videoed me placing the foam finger, which is what makes the video so spectacular now.

Brandon enjoyed the tree so much that he insisted we leave it up until we had to move at the end of the school year. He also let me know that he wanted to help decorate it again the next Christmas, even though he wouldn't be living with me.

A group of us took a picture in front of the tree when we threw a small party on Brandon's twenty-first birthday. It wasn't really much of a party, with just a few of us hanging out. We just didn't want Brandon's birthday to go by unnoticed. The main thing that came from that night was the picture. We all wore the shirt that Sigma Chi sold in memory of Brandon and posed in ways that Brandon had for memorable pictures. Oh, and I also slid into my future wife's DMs for the first time that night, but that's for later.

There are a lot of things that'll be with me forever through losing Brandon: the friends from that night, his family, the memories, my wife, and the tattoo on my left shoulder blade. A tattoo is another way we tend to remember a lost loved one. It's something that's with you forever, a symbol of how we want our memory of them to last. It seemed like a friend of Brandon's was getting tatted almost every day at the time.

For anyone that really knows me, the fact I actually have a tattoo is kind of absurd. To be honest, I'm kind of a wimp. Tattoos are more for tough guys or the carefree people who don't think about the consequences of everything they do. I'm the opposite of both of those.

When I was young, I talked about getting a tattoo because all the professional wrestlers I watched on WWE were tatted up. That desire was over by high school. My mom told me she never really worried about my want to get all those tattoos when I was little because she knew how I was, and that when the time really came, I wouldn't have it in me.

Brandon had wanted a tattoo since the day I met him and tried to talk me into getting one with him since then, too. I always had an excuse not to.

"What if I don't like what I got years from now?"

"What if it looks bad when I'm old and wrinkly?"

"Well, I can't have one where a potential employer might see it."

Brandon was persistent, though. He eventually got one without me. He went home one weekend sophomore year, then returned with the Texas state outline tattooed on his forearm. I knew it was coming eventually because of how much he talked about it, but I had no idea he was getting it that weekend. I'm not sure when he knew he was really getting it either.

That tattoo just broke the barrier, making Brandon want more ink. He and Gloria even left my house one night with a plan to get tattoos. They would have gotten one, too, if there had been any tattoo shops open in Stillwater past 10 p.m. on a weekday.

I eventually made a deal with Brandon that I would get one with him for our twenty-first birthdays, which were less than a month apart. My plan was that would hold him off for a while and give me more time for another excuse. I did really want one, but those excuses I mentioned earlier were always in the back of my mind, keeping me from just going for it.

I never got a chance to give Brandon another excuse, though. Plus, a deal's a deal. Losing Brandon also gave me that "Live every day like it's your last" mentality, so here was the time to not think about how I feel about something permanent years from now.

While most "In Memory" tattoos I looked at had the date someone died, or their birthday and the day they died, I didn't really care for either of those days. I obviously wasn't there the day he was born. The day I lost him was probably the worst day of my life, so why would I want something on my body constantly reminding me of that time? I decided to remember the day we met: July 2, 2014. That was the day Brandon took that first step by reaching out and starting the whole journey. If there was a day that should be more important than the others in our friendship, it would be then.

The date is in the middle of the phrase, "Loyal and True."

"Loyal and true" is part of OSU's alma mater, which fans sing at least once at every Cowboy sporting event. It's something Brandon and I always talked about doing one last time as students together at graduation one day. He was usually the one next to me at sporting events who I put my arm around as the rest of the crowd also put their arms around their neighbor's shoulder and lightly swayed back and forth.

The twist to the phrase is what Brandon enjoyed most. As the song goes, "Ever you'll find us loyal and true," the student section screams "SO TRUE!" at the top of their lungs. That was Brandon's favorite part of the alma-mater. He once sat with his friends in the Texas Tech student section when OSU played football in Lubbock, Texas, and while he kept his mouth shut and his jacket zipped the whole game, he couldn't help himself during the alma-mater when the game concluded with a Cowboy victory.

After a road win, standing in the middle of thousands of angry Texas Tech fans, Brandon unzipped his jacket to unveil a bright orange shirt as he yelled, "SO TRUE!" as the Cowboy Marching Band played the tune.

That story, and the phrase, just epitomizes everything about Brandon. He was the most loyal and the truest man I've ever known. To his university, to his family, to his friends. Brandon Cavazos was "Loyal and True."

Chapter 10

I thought I recognized the name. My phone had been blowing up the days and hours after Brandon's death, with people sharing their condolences, telling me they were praying for me, and asking if I needed anything. I either knew who the person was, or didn't at all and assumed it was one of Brandon's relatives or friends. Some of the people I didn't know sounded familiar from stories I had heard from Brandon.

A girl reached out to me on Facebook to not only state her condolences but also share pictures she had of me and Brandon. She was the only one to do such a thing, and I assumed others had plenty of other pictures considering how much Brandon enjoyed taking selfies, especially if I was caught off-guard or looked goofy in the background. I hope I at least thanked her for the pictures. I had so many people reaching out at the time I was just constantly typing, "Thanks. Love you too." I wish I could explain now to every single person that contacted me how much their support still means to me today. It was just hard to express that emotion at the time and keep up with everyone.

I had so many strangers who knew of me through Brandon and wanted to reach out that I just started accepting every friend request I got on Facebook if Brandon was a mutual friend. That's how I connected with this particular girl. She also followed me on Twitter like many others, and her name kept popping up in my notifications because she was "liking" things I tweeted. Granted, most of my tweets at the time involved Brandon, which is why she was interacting with me so much. That interaction caused me to creep some on her profile, though, and after seeing her profile picture, I knew she was my type.

I still remember the picture perfectly. At first glance, I thought she was probably out of my league. She definitely was. And still is. Every guy has a dream girl envisioned in their brain. Mine was blonde with light blue eyes. That was exactly this girl. She was wearing a black dress and an awkward smile while posing in front of a mirror for this picture.

I always thought about how I wanted to have a good story to tell my kids one day about how I met their mother. A lot of parents even make up a story because they don't want to tell their children they met drunk at a bar. My generation's version of that is social media. I really didn't want to ever have to tell my kids that I slid into their mom's DMs because I thought she looked good in her profile picture. But, on December 10, 2016, I slid into my future children's mom's DMs at 3:11 in the morning.

I was probably going off adrenaline and liquid courage after celebrating Brandon's twenty-first birthday at my house. It was the same night a group of us took that picture with matching navy blue long-sleeve shirts. When the night eventually ended and I finally checked my phone, I had another notification about "Spark" "liking" one of my tweets. Her username was "Spark" from the combination of her first and last name, Sara Park. Today, "Sgregory" doesn't have a very good ring to it. The name didn't ring much of a bell, though. I had completely forgotten about the conversation with Brandon on the way back from the Colvin sophomore year about the Sara Park girl who was wife material and I'd just ruin my chances with then.

First, I would like to apologize that a blog and a book, as well as my entire marriage, are pretty much based on this over-hyped DM. The first words sent to my future wife were, "I can always count on you for a like, LOL." And at 3:24 in the morning, SHE RESPONDED. From all the miracles that took place to get me and Sara together, I think the fact she didn't ignore me is the craziest of all. Here's another letdown, though. That conversation actually went nowhere. She responded, I responded, she responded again, then it ended. We didn't talk again for thirteen days.

I obviously wanted to talk to her more, but my dilemma was how to DM her again, out of the blue, without making it seem too random, or like I was some creep that thought she was pretty (which I did). Sliding into someone's DMs already seems creepy enough. I spent the next thirteen days thinking of either the perfect reason that required a DM or the right words to say. I came up with neither.

Sara had a thing back then that she would add festive emojis that related to whatever upcoming season or holiday to her name on Twitter. I messaged her again on December 23, two days before Christmas, so the emojis were Christmas trees and Santa or something. I asked her, since Christmas was coming to an end, what emojis she was going to add to her name next, probably followed by a "LOL." It took me thirteen days to come up with that. But in my defense, a week of that time was devoted to studying and taking finals. Maybe my thought process was still lagging from finals week, influencing the terrible decision.

Nonetheless, for some reason, Sara responded again. Awkward small talk and jokes were made, eventually leading to me bringing up that I was watching Elf, which happens to be one of Sara's all-time favorite movies. And not just favorite Christmas movie, I mean one of her favorite movies to watch no matter the season. We just had our first Christmas together as a married couple, and we watched Elf nine times, and then once more after the holidays.

Then, somehow, for some reason, a strand of Elf gifs started from the both of us. And I'm not talking just a few. You could scroll and scroll through our conversation, and you'd just see Will Ferrell again and again.

The goofiness of us both was evident. That's probably the first common trait that made us have a connection. It led to the Elf gifs, which eventually ended with me getting Sara's number later that day. Well, I didn't actually get her number. I made the rookie mistake of giving her my digits and telling her to text me. I gave this girl way out of my league the chance to either text me or never talk to me again. The only reason I even did that much was because Pud, the best man at our wedding, bet that I couldn't get her number after I told him about this new girl. That was after I showed him a picture of Sara, and he laughed about my chances with her.

Like Brandon (the two are actually a lot alike), Pud knew how to get me to step out of my comfort zone. I've known Pud since sixth grade, and he's forced me into uncomfortable situations ever since. However, most of the time, (not always) it's because he knows it's something I really want to do or should do, I'm just not bold enough on my own.

Pud is even the one who counseled me and led me to the Lord at a church camp. He was a student leader who had to go upfront at the end of every service to talk to other kids who either wanted to take a step of faith, or just needed someone to listen. It was something I eventually did alongside Pud a few years later, but that never would have been possible without Pud's guidance. That night, only hours after I had started my new walk with Christ, Pud put me on the spot and made me share my testimony right there in front of our whole cabin. I was furious with him at the moment, but since then, sharing my testimony has been so easy considering I've done it since literally my first moments as a Christian.

Being three years older, Pud's always been like a big brother looking after me. But also like an older brother, he's not going to get sappy and make it look obvious that he's trying to help me.

Sara texted me almost as quick as she could have saved my number in her contacts. I immediately gave her a hard time for not following the old-fashioned "three-day rule," especially after I waited thirteen days to reach out a second time. However, by day three, I probably would have thought I ruined my chance with her like Brandon predicted, although Brandon was just waiting for the perfect situation to connect me and Sara. Apparently, this was the perfect time for us.

I don't think there was a moment I was awake, during the holiday season, I wasn't texting Sara. We had technically known about each other for a while—Sara more than me—but had been actually acquainted for less than a month. Despite that, there was never a lull in a conversation. We were already bonding through deep talks and sharing our emotions, which I rarely ever do, and still don't.

Once Christmas was over, I had a trip planned to San Antonio to cover OSU in the Alamo Bowl for the O'Colly. I still talked to Sara between a busy schedule, and she spent most of our conversations telling me to be careful while I explored a new city.

Traveling for free to sporting events and new places was one of the coolest parts of my time at the O'Colly. Considering my life centered on work at the time and my job revolved around sports, sports were usually about eighty percent of my talking points. That's what I knew best and felt most comfortable discussing. I also thought I had a pretty cool job, and so did others, so I could always brag a little about what I did in conversations. Sara had zero interest in the sports world, though, which, for as much as we talked, took a big toll on my conversation starters.

Any event I bragged about attending, it didn't matter to her because she had no idea if it was important or not. While Sara and I were dating, I talked to an Olympic gold medalist on a weekly basis, had a moment with NBA All-Star, Allen Iverson, sat down with NFL Hall of Famer, Steve Largent, and talked to countless other legends in the sports world. Of all those, Sara (and her mom) have cared about only one encounter I had: Ice Cube. All I did was shake his hand and quickly ask him a few questions in less than two minutes before a Big3 Basketball event. Yes, Ice Cube is cool, but c'mon, that same day, Allen Iverson literally put his arm over my shoulder and walked me to the locker room while he told me about his first NBA Summer League season. Sara just said, "That's neat," after I told her about my A.I. experience. Then she asked me how tall Ice Cube is in person.

I've been beyond blessed with the opportunities I've been given through my career, with the people I've met and places I've been, and at one point I tended to brag about those experiences a lot. It was a huge deal to me, but Sara quickly humbled me when none of it seemed exciting to her, no matter how hard she tried to fake a worthy reaction. She still tries to act overjoyed today, but I can easily tell when it's an act and she really has no idea what I'm talking about.

Even though I already knew at this point that Sara didn't care about sports or my job, I thought I finally had a way through work to impress her. I didn't get to do this because of who I was or anything; I just knew the right person. I sometimes made guest appearances on an Oklahoma sports radio station. I was scheduled to go on the morning before the Alamo Bowl for about ten minutes, which is how long I was usually on. It would obviously sound like a different language to Sara if she listened, but my family and I thought me being on the radio was the coolest thing ever, so I thought surely she might, too.

I mentioned it to Sara, but not like, "Hey, you should listen."

I was all cool, like, "Yeah, I gotta go do this radio thing in a bit. No big deal, I don't pee my pants every time I'm on air or anything."

Sara, of course, asked how she could listen. I pretended like I didn't really want her to tune in but still sent her the online link. She listened while having no idea what the host and I were discussing. I thought I had made an impression, but I later found out, since we had only texted up to that point, Sara just wanted to hear my voice to see if it sounded annoying or learn if I had a bad hick accent.

Despite not being able to talk about eighty percent of my knowledge, Sara and I never had trouble sparking a new conversation, though. My first night back in Stillwater after that San Antonio trip, we Facetimed for the first time. Sara had been requesting for a while, but I absolutely hated Facetime, and I'm still not a big fan of it, even though it became a daily thing while Sara and I were dating long-distance. That first call lasted almost four hours. We just rambled. I probably told Sara more about myself that night than I had most people I knew most of my life. We didn't even realize how long we had been on the phone until we hung up and the time popped up. From that point on, a week didn't go by in my life without Facetiming Sara at least once a week, usually more, until we eventually got married and lived together (spoiler alert).

When I hung up from that first Facetime call, it actually reminded me of Brandon, with how quickly we clicked. Sara and I still talk about how it feels like we've known each other our whole lives, and like we've been together most of that time. I felt the same way about Brandon. It's crazy to think I knew Brandon for only about three and a half years, but he still made an impact on me that will last a lifetime.

I wouldn't even know my wife if it wasn't for him, but yet, she's been part of my life even longer than he physically was.

Chapter 11

This is honestly when my life became less entertaining. Freshman year, Brandon would always say that we needed our own TV series. We thought it seemed like a great idea until it dawned on us that something being on TV means anyone can watch it, including our grandmas. We really didn't want our grandmas seeing the trouble we were getting into.

But by senior year, my stresses were less about drinking too much and failing a test, and more about finding a job and planning a wedding. My last year in college definitely wouldn't have had the same comedic script as that first. It was probably because all the dumb moments and mistakes began to disappear after I started dating Sara. I had always heard people say that some troubled boy needed to find a good girl to straighten up and settle down. I always thought that was just a saying until I actually did straighten up and settle down after meeting a good girl.

Sara made a trip to Stillwater right before that winter break we first started talking ended. We know it sounds crazy now, and both thought it seemed absurd then, too. We had been talking for less than a month, but now Sara was already driving four hours to a different state to meet me. It was a leap of faith for both of us, but an even bigger one for Sara. She says she wouldn't have taken that trip if it wasn't for Brandon, trusting his judgment that I really was a good guy and she'd be safe visiting Stillwater to meet me.

I would have driven that first trip, but I had my own place in Stillwater, and Sara was still living with her parents. A four-drive didn't seem worth a quick dinner and movie before heading right back to Oklahoma. Plus, it'd probably throw things a little off to meet parents at the same time as actually meeting the girl.

It's been over three years since then, and we still can't believe that trip was even possible for Sara. Even though Sara was an adult in college, she still lived as if she was a high schooler under her parents' roof. She still had to ask permission before she did anything or went anywhere. And Sara didn't have the type of father that routinely said yes, either. I obviously didn't know this at the time, being used to interacting with other college students free to do whatever they wanted hours away from their guardians.

The more I know Sara's dad, the more insane it seems that he actually let his daughter drive to Stillwater to meet a boy he didn't know. He barely let Sara sleepover at a friend's house in the same town, let alone stay with a boy in a different state. That was definitely one of those small miracles that had to take place to get me and Sara together.

No matter how it happened, though, I got to take Sara out for sweet-peppered bacon cheese fries. Eskimo Joe's is a staple in Stillwater, so I knew that was where I had to take Sara on our first date, as part of OSU student tradition. Famous for its cheese fries and T-shirts, Eskimo Joe's also has a great atmosphere, but is far from romantic. I could barely comprehend romance, though, and still don't. However, on our first Valentine's Day together, I planned a scavenger hunt for Sara that ended at a nearby park with a small lake for a picnic with me and sweet-peppered bacon cheese fries from Eskimo Joe's.

Sara eventually got burnt out on cheese fries and isn't the biggest fan of Eskimo Joe's today. However, we still have to eat there every time we're in Stillwater. Like it's a staple in Stillwater, Eskimo Joe's became iconic in our relationship, as well, because of that first date.

The restaurant is also known for its cups you get to take home when you order a drink with your meal. The cups come in an endless amount of colors on its famous large-rimmed look with a logo on both sides. They're like fine china in Stillwater, filling college students' cabinets and making beer pong games much easier with their large opening. Those same cups also now sit in the cabinets of our closest friends and family after we ordered over two hundred of them to be the drinkware at our wedding reception in honor of our first date. Just like visiting Eskimo Joe's, every wedding guest took home a souvenir cup. We also ended up with all the extras, so we drink from only Joe's cups now. We have so many that our grandkids will also probably be sipping juice from a glow-in-the-dark Eskimo Joe's cup from our wedding.

I had planned to take things as slow as possible with Sara. I was a little over a year from graduating college and had no idea where I'd end up with my career. I always figured I'd be sort of a nomad after I graduated college, taking any job I desired, no matter where it was because I would be a free man. Because of that, I didn't think a serious relationship was the best idea with so much change coming. A stable relationship usually doesn't stay intact with so much instability around it. Not to mention the distance. Sara and I lived four hours apart in different states. I had never heard of a long-distance relationship actually working out, especially since I figured we'd still be away from each other even after college graduation because of our career goals.

I didn't listen to myself, though, thankfully. Before Sara even drove back to Texas the next day on her first visit, we were official. It was probably the first life decision I ever made without my career at the forefront. Sara and I were lying there talking when I blurted out, "You think we can really make this work?"

Sara just answered, "Yes," and that was good enough for me. I tend to blurt things out like that when I'm nervous about the response. I did the same thing the first time I told Sara I loved her.

My heart dropped when Sara responded, "What?" But she really had no idea what I had just said because I didn't even take a breath between my mumble. She eventually said it back after finally realizing what I said.

Sara and I drove that four-hour stretch on I-35 between Stillwater and Bedford countless times the next year and a half, making sure to see each other at least one weekend every month. I met her parents the first time I made that trek and had to stay with them since that's where Sara still lived. Having nothing but negative comments to say about all Sara's previous boyfriends, Sara's dad surprisingly said only positive things to her after my first visit. My mom is just as picky, thinking none of my past girlfriends quite lived up to the expectations she had for her son, which were almost impossible to live up to for any high school girl. However, she loved Sara after our first visit together to Locust Grove. Sara was actually the first time I got immediate approval for a girl from my mom.

I fell more and more in love with Sara every trip. I had thought a companion like Brandon was irreplaceable, and Sara could never actually replace Brandon, but I once again had a best friend who I could share everything with and endure life with. However, even though I was enjoying every moment with Sara, craving the next, I still wasn't sure how long it would last. I was almost sure there was an end. I knew I loved her, but I was still selfish, questioning if she was worth making "me" an "us," and letting her possibly interfere with the plans I had for myself. Then I almost lost her.

I was in the middle of a nap when Sara's mom called me for the third time. Sara was on her way up to Locust Grove to celebrate Independence Day with my family. She never made it that weekend, though.

It was supposed to be our first weekend with the little Gregory family we were starting to create. I was extremely busy with my Tulsa World internship that summer, so Sara was making most of the trips back and forth. During Sara's previous visit, I somehow ended up with a puppy. He was ours, not just mine, though, which meant things were getting pretty serious.

Sara and I were actually having a difficult time in our relationship when we found Tooter Bean. I honestly wasn't putting forth all my effort into the relationship thinking it had an expiration date. Our honeymoon phase had ended, and I think the long-distance was taking a toll on us, especially with how busy work was keeping me.

Sara has a heart of gold and is obsessed with dogs, so when Syd, whose mom lives a block away from my dad, posted that she rescued some puppies, Sara said we had to go see them. I was expecting dogs, not puppies. I was also expecting just to go pet them and let Sara see them, not bring one home.

We both immediately knew we needed Tooter, though, even as I kept making excuses. I had set some unrealistic guidelines for Sara a few weeks before when she was trying to talk me into getting a dog. I said I wanted to rescue one, but a puppy, not a dog. I also wanted a Dachshund, like I had when I was little, but I also wanted it mixed with another breed.

Sara must have prayed hard. A three-pound mixed Dachshund puppy was drinking from a bowl of water when we walked up to Syd's porch. He was brown with a white chest, with multiple patches of fur missing. He darted his big brown eyes at us, with the white of his eyes peeking through the corner. He still gives us the same look today to get what he wants.

Syd rescued him and his siblings from someone's front yard. His owners had the puppies outside, with their kids picking the puppies up by their limbs and throwing them around like stuffed animals. Syd confronted the owners. They just told her they didn't even want the puppies, so Syd scooped them up and said she'd find them a better home.

Sara sat on the ground picking fleas off the only puppy left as she begged me to claim him. He ended up spending the day with us, and we just haven't returned him to Syd yet almost two years later.

The puppy was perfect, other than his constant gas. The sudden change of diet did a number on his stomach, making this tiny animal stink up a room. Sara had always wanted a dog named "Bean," but this one was clearly a "Tooter." That's how Tooter Bean got his name and became the glue of the Gregory family.

Tooter was exactly what we needed to keep us together at the time. That Fourth of July was going to be the first time we were all together since Sara had to go back to Texas the day after we got Tooter. She even had a red, white, and blue bandana for Tooter to wear, which he still wore Independence Day to match my socks.

Sara never made it to me and Tooter that weekend, though. A semi crashed into the side of Sara's tiny Honda Civic while merging, forcing the car to spin off the highway at over seventy miles per hour. It bounced off the steel bumpers in the median while still spinning for about twenty yards. Sara's car was totaled, mangled with no window unbroken and seemingly every inch dented. But Sara was fine. She miraculously had only whiplash and a few cuts. She was sore, but alive.

The wreck happened just over halfway between Bedford and Locust Grove, an hour-longer trip than to Stillwater. I raced to the hospital the ambulance took her to, still not fully sure what happened or how she was. At this point, someone at the scene had only told Sara's parents their daughter was in an accident, then Sara's mom relayed the message to me.

The blood on Sara was dried by the time I got to her. She was sitting in a hospital room barely able to move because of soreness. She was more shaken up than anything, though. And the most upsetting part for her was having to be alone the two hours before I got there.

Even though Sara was alive, I saw her laying in that hospital bed and thought about how the next time I saw Brandon after a phone call like that he was lying in a coffin at his funeral. That could have also been Sara. I felt like I had almost lost another best friend. It forced me to think about my life without Sara. It became obvious that it was something I never wanted.

Sara's parents eventually met us after a longer drive. On their way back to Texas, Sara's dad said that I proved my love for Sara that day. In my mind, I hadn't done anything too special. I thought any decent human would have rushed to the hospital to take care of a loved one after being told they were in an accident.

Her dad was right, though. I had proved my love for Sara to myself. It was the moment I realized I didn't ever want a life without Sara by my side. I didn't ask Sara to marry me or anything that day, but I did tell her I fully planned on marrying her. I had already lost Brandon, so I was going to do anything in my power to make sure I never lost her, too.

I asked Sara to be my wife that November, a day before Thanksgiving. We both knew it was coming, so it wasn't much of a surprise to her. She even helped pick out the ring because I wanted to make sure I didn't get one she didn't actually like. Sara didn't know it was happening that particular day, though, no matter what she says today.

My mom is a photographer on the side, and Sara always dreamt of taking Fall pictures, so we had plans to while we were down for Thanksgiving. The only instruction I ever got from Sara about how to propose was that she wanted someone there to capture the moment. That made this photo session with my mom seem like the best opportunity.

Everything fell into place perfectly, and honestly pretty last-minute. We had ordered two rings for Sara to try on, but since I knew which one she really liked more (the more expensive one, of course), I was going to snag that one without her knowing. The only problem was that there was a chance the ring wouldn't arrive on time. Sara had already made it to Stillwater to spend her Thanksgiving break in Oklahoma, so because the ring hadn't arrived yet, I also had to try and pick up the ring without her knowing, if it even arrived before we left for Locust Grove. Luckily, I got a call from the jewelry store the morning we were planning to leave that the ring was in. I hustled down to the jewelry store and bought it immediately. Our photo session was scheduled for the next day.

I had to kick things into gear now, but I'm a sports journalist so I work best on deadline. The first step was officially getting her dad's blessing. My original plan was to do this during my next visit to Texas, but that was before this new masterplan I had devised. I hated not doing it in-person, but I called her dad in the jewelry store parking lot, explaining that I hated doing it over the phone, but everything was just falling into place perfectly. He approved, and getting Sara's dad's blessing was a big deal for Sara, so I knew her thinking I hadn't done this yet (or having a chance to) would leave Sara oblivious.

I then dropped the bomb on my mom, giving her about twenty-four hours to arrange the most important photoshoot she had ever done. I kind of threw her to the wolves, with no real plan for the photoshoot other than I was going to propose at some point. We tried to arrange some kind of cue to signal when I was going to propose moments before, but apparently, neither of us knew the cue, so she was just awkwardly taking us to new spots, pretending to snap pictures as she waited for me to get down on one knee.

I managed to keep the ring hidden in a small pocket of my backpack for the next day, paranoid the whole time, wanting to check on it every few minutes as if it'd grow legs and hitchhike back to the jewelry store. The problem was that I wasn't going to take the backpack to the photoshoot, but I still had to take the ring out of the bag, and then transport it to where we were taking pictures without Sara noticing it.

Per Sara's request, Tooter was part of our photoshoot, spending most of the time in my younger sister's arms. My sister videoed me proposing, but the frame is diagonal and constantly shifting because she was trying to be a director and dog sitter at the same time, while also trying to be sneaky.

I pretended to forget Tooter's treats, a necessity for him to behave, giving me a reason to go back inside without Sara to get the ring out of the bag and into my back pocket. Sara swears she knew something was up by this time, thinking I had hidden the ring in Tooter's treat bag. That honestly would have been smarter. Instead, I sat on one cheek the whole drive, trying not to smash the ring box and also avoid the discomfort of sitting on it. Sara says she was alerted a proposal might be possible after my dad left the house, and instead of saying "Good-bye," he yelled, "Good luck!" as he walked out the door.

I thought I wouldn't be nervous. I knew Sara would say yes, so why should I be? But the moment we stepped out of the car and arrived at the spot where I planned to make Sara my fiancé, I started to panic. I think it was more of wanting everything to go perfect for her, especially since I put everything together so quickly. I just kept imagining the worst, like Tooter running off to chase a squirrel, making Sara cry as we spent the next hour searching for him in the woods.

I kept putting the actual proposal off, and every time my mom darted her eyes at me, trying not to let Sara see, but also making sure I got the message to do it already. I was waiting for the perfect spot, though, and also questioning if this was a good enough spot and time to even do it at all. I finally felt like this spot had the best backdrop, as we stood on a rocky cliff with a creek running through the green grass and red, fallen leaves behind us. I just said exactly what I was thinking.

"This would be a good spot to propose."

"What?" Sara giggled. It was like the first time I told her I loved her all over again.

I didn't know what else to say, forgetting to plan some romantic speech, so I just knelt down and pulled out the ring. Sara immediately asked if I had asked her dad, and when, and a handful of other questions before realizing she hadn't actually said yes yet. I then tried to put the ring on the wrong hand and finger before Sara corrected me. Sara cried as she hugged me, so did my mom, and I tried not to.

That was the biggest moment of our lives at the time. It's not anymore, but because of that, we've been by each other's side for every monumental event since: graduating from college, getting our first real job, our wedding. And we still have more to come as our time together, and family, are sure to grow even more.

Chapter 12

I couldn't take my eyes off Sara as she walked down the gravel aisle through rows of our closest friends and relatives, her dad latched onto her left side. Her dad was there as part of tradition, needing to give his daughter away, but also for support as Sara tried to balance in her heels on the tiny gray rocks while one hand also helped hold up the bottom of her white dress.

I never took my eyes off Sara during her stroll down that aisle. I didn't even hear "Here Comes the Bride" playing over the speaker, or notice the reactions of the maybe one hundred people standing on both sides of her. I just watched as Sara looked down every few steps to make sure she wasn't going to fall, but mainly keeping her eyes locked on mine as we both beamed.

Most of those in attendance were probably distracted by the scenery behind me. It was a picture most, especially those from Texas, couldn't believe existed in Oklahoma. Some of those from Locust Grove didn't even know such scenery was in their own backyard. The bright green hills rolled to the blue sky behind the tall wooden cross standing between two rock walls, which at this point were hidden behind young adults dressed in tuxes and dresses as part of their friend's wedding ceremony. Those twelve were probably looking at the reactions of others in the crowd in front of them, or making sure the ring bearer and flower girl were behaving on the stage. Most of my groom's party was trying to see if I had any tears welling from my eyes yet because bets on me crying were placed in the tiny room before.

I was oblivious to the close friends and beautiful scenery behind me, though. For probably the first time in my life, I was focused on what was right in front of me at the present moment. I was in awe of my gorgeous bride. But because of what was behind us, which might not have seemed as elegant as our current background, that past somehow made this moment, and the future it was about to start, possible.

I got to the wedding venue early that day. The wedding wasn't supposed to start until five that evening in hopes the June heat would cool down by then. We were wrong in that assumption. My groomsmen and I had it the worst, wearing a jacket and layered tux with the sun beating down on the cement we were standing on.

I had plenty of time but still woke up early, getting breakfast with one of my groomsmen. I then went to the church, where Big Mama was cooking for the two hundred projected guests. Big Mama insisted she wanted to prepare the meal—pasta and salad—for the reception. I wanted to make sure she didn't need anything from me during crunch time. My family is absolutely incredible, though, and was already helping her so I wasn't really needed. I had aunts scurrying around the church's kitchen before the wedding and during the reception to help Big Mama, and my cousin, Misty, who was baking the cake and cupcakes.

The only other place left for me to go was the wedding venue, where all the girls were already putting makeup on, and my and Sara's parents were sprinting around the area trying to accomplish everything that needed to be done before they had to get dressed themselves. Sara's dad had said yes to doing just about every available job for the day of. He had sweat pouring from his hat when I walked up. He rattled off a list of tasks he needed to complete, then away he went.

The girls had overtaken the room reserved for the guys to get ready. It was just a tiny room with cement walls, three empty beds, and a body-length mirror borrowed from my younger sister's bedroom. I went ahead and just stashed my tux and backpack in the kitchen area, where we were supposed to wait until the girls cleared out of our area. The kitchen had A/C so it was much better than standing outside.

I admired our scenery only once that day. I was the only one outside for a moment after Sara's dad left, so I walked to where the ceremony would take place a few hours later. I paused at the start of the aisle and brown benches. It was like I was walking the field before a state championship game. I even said a prayer at the center alter at the end of the aisle (the end zone), where I would eventually say, "I do." I not only asked God to help that day go smoothly, but I knew I needed his help and guidance, and still do, to be the husband Sara deserves.

That's honestly probably the last time I felt alone. I've obviously been by myself since, just usually with dogs close by. But that seemed like the last time I was actually alone, even without my phone, which might as well be like having the world's population in your pocket.

Daniel, who I got breakfast with that morning, was the first of my groomsmen to show up shortly after my prayer ended. They started filing in one-by-one then, as we soon migrated and staked our claim to our tiny concrete room, where we helped each other tie ties and adjust cufflinks. I wore special cufflinks that Ms. Cavazos got me as a gift. One held a picture of me and Brandon while the other had that famous image of Brandon posing in the fountain at OSU. Sara and I tried any way possible to make it feel like Brandon was present at our wedding, even though Ms. Cavazos, who attended, repeatedly told us not to feel obligated to honor Brandon in any way. We wanted to, though.

I mainly wanted to feel Brandon's presence to ease my nerves. Brandon used to carry around a poker chip that he would play with between his fingers. Ms. Cavazos ordered some bright-orange poker chips after Brandon's death and handed them out to some of his friends. I don't even remember actually getting it, but I came across the poker chip the night before the wedding. It was in my pocket all day, as I twiddled it between my fingers to keep my mind busy and nerves at ease. I never even told anyone I had it, just keeping it hidden in my pocket.

At the reception, Pud mentioned in his speech that Brandon should have had Pud's title as Best Man, not him. I never wanted Pud to feel like some sort of replacement. He was more deserving of that role than he'll ever know. I give him the credit for being the key factor in why my groom's party clicked so well and had such great

131

experiences, from the bachelor party, to even decorating the night before.

We joked even after my wedding that from then on it had to be that same group for everyone's wedding because we all clicked so well. It's kind of nerve-racking to assemble a group of friends like that, especially when they come from the different stages of your life. I think most at least knew of each other beforehand, either from high school, or visits to Stillwater, or going to OSU, as well.

My party included Syd as a groom's lady. She was still part of everything just like one of the guys. With Pud as my Best Man, Daniel, Braden, KJ, and Marshall completed those by my side, not only for my wedding, but so much more before and since.

Marshall and I had been close friends for only about a year. We had known each other since freshman year through working for the O'Colly but never really bonded until later. He became somewhat of my right-hand man senior year, though.

The rest of my party took advantage of Marshall not knowing me very well for that long. Without me knowing, the group was placing bets, such as moments I would cry. Marshall was the only one to lose money on this particular bet. The rest had apparently seen my sensitivity before and knew tears would escape during my first look with Sara. They used Sara's Maid of Honor as a spy to tell them if I cried or not. I technically didn't cry, only had a few tears, so I hope Marshall didn't completely lose that bet.

Tooter was also part of our wedding, of course, carried down the aisle by my younger sister. There were running bets on if Tooter would pee, run off, or bark during the ceremony. Tooter wore a doggy diaper and was too scared to misbehave, so those who didn't have faith in Tooter Bean lost that one.

One of my uncles, who's a preacher, officiated our wedding, like he's done dozens of times before. He said we not only had the first wedding he's attended with a groom's lady, but it was also the first time he had seen a dog be part of a ceremony.

Despite all the factors, nothing went wrong on our wedding day. Well, if it did, we didn't mind it, anyway. Sara and I had decided before that we would not stress on the actual day so we could enjoy it as much as possible. However, the week leading up to the big day had us wanting to just elope.

Actually, I'm probably the only one who screwed up, at least during the ceremony. During our vows, my uncle asked me to repeat, "God richly *blessed* me with..."

Instead, I said, "God richly *breast* me with..."

Sara, of course, started laughing because I said, "breast." Then she couldn't stop as she bent over with laughter. That just made the congregation continue to cackle. And all that did was just prolong my embarrassing mishap, which at this time, I didn't even know what I said. I thought I had just stuttered a bit. My groomsmen told me what I said when the ceremony was over. I thought they were lying, but, of course, there was video to not only prove what I said, but also document my miswording and post it to social media.

The show went on, though. The wedding wouldn't have epitomized my and Sara's relationship if it wasn't a good time. We're both goofier than we should be, so our wedding was, too. All that mattered is if we said, "I do," which we did after I finally got the right words out. I even swooped her down for our first kiss. I was told I should have warned Sara and the photographer that I planned to do that, but to be honest, I didn't know what I was doing until I was actually doing it. It made for an incredible picture, though, which is still the wallpaper on my phone today.

We walked away after that kiss. We walked back down the aisle, this time together, and eventually, after the reception and more pictures, to our own life together. I imagine that's when my and Sara's relationship becomes just like anyone else's. We moved in together. We got another dog, Bruno. We started new jobs. Dekota and Sara became the Gregorys. It's crazy how two people really do just seem to become the same person, just like that.

I lived with Ms. Cavazos in Bedford the weeks leading up to the wedding, when Sara and I still had different last names. I was staying in Brandon's room, the first to do so since his death. I had to move to the area after graduation because of a job, which I quit in three days (different story for a different time). I didn't move in with Sara since she still lived with her parents, and we also wanted to wait until we were married to actually live together, mainly because my mom and Ms. Cavazos wouldn't have it any other way.

During that time is when I started writing my own story for the first time. I started a blog to, honestly, selfishly vent my emotions, because writing is really the only way I know how to. I also wanted to document my memories with Brandon before more details started to slip.

The blog caused some of Brandon's friends to reach out to me, telling me how my stories had forced them to remember their times with Brandon they thought they had forgotten. Every single one of their stories were different. That started my hope that others would start to share their own story. If mine could help someone, surely yours could, too.

As I started writing this book, I dove back into studying the Bible on a daily basis, reading it every morning with a cup of coffee. I had done this before, usually during a tough time, or when I needed answers about something. It was usually short-lived, though, and selfish, because I was only hoping it would benefit me somehow.

The week I actually finished the first draft of the book, my eyes were drawn to the story of when Jesus healed a blind man in John, chapter nine. It wasn't even part of the devotion I was going through at the time. It's also a story I've read or heard dozens of times while growing up in church, but I guess I never really paid attention.

When the disciples saw the blind man, they assumed his disability was a consequence of his or his parents' sins. Jesus told them his blindness wasn't a consequence of anything, it was just part of that man's story, saying, "This happened so that the works of God might be displayed in him."

Jesus then healed the blind man by rubbing mud on the man's eyes and telling him to go wash it off. The blind man could see once the mud was rinsed away. He went back home, and, of course, everyone immediately noticed the man could now see. As they asked why, the man was pretty much forced to tell them about Jesus and what he can do.

I was like the blind man after I lost Brandon. I'm honestly still like the blind man most of the time. I couldn't see what was ahead of me, and although I wanted to trust that God had a reason to end Brandon's life so soon, it was hard to fathom an outcome great enough. I couldn't imagine any good coming from such a situation.

My story really didn't seem very powerful to me. It didn't sound like much when I said my friend died. It's not like I had lost a child or a parent, or any family for that matter. But I realized everyone has a friend. As sad as it seems, reality is that not everyone has a parent, or a child, or a sibling, or even a family. In a way, we could count them lucky, because that's someone they won't have to handle losing. Or worry about losing. I still sometimes imagine people I love dying. I don't purposely do it, it's just like my mind is subconsciously trying to prepare me for the possibility.

Everyone has a friend, though. And my best friend died. A haunting, gruesome sentence to type, yes. A phrase that still has consequences, like constantly worrying about the possibility of others dying too soon. Or what we believe is too soon.

I sometimes feel ashamed that Brandon was put on this earth only to benefit my life. That's obviously not true, even though I do sometimes feel guilty about the blessings I've gained as a result of his death. I saw a room full of people at Brandon's funeral, though, that assured me that my life wasn't the only one impacted because of Brandon. My wife couldn't have been the only soul saved that day.

Whether you believe in God or not, there has to be a higher entity involved to make all this happen. I don't believe stars just align on their own. My faith has me sure that God is the only reason I met Brandon Cavazos on July

2, 2014. God is the reason why I married Sara Park on June 16, 2018.

Somehow, a boy from Locust Grove, Oklahoma, met a girl, and a best friend, from Bedford, Texas. That might make this a love story. I'm not sure it really is, though. I would say it's more about overcoming the loss of a friend and discovering God always has a plan. But friends can love each other, too, and God definitely loves us. So call it what you want.

I've told thousands of stories, and I finally shared my own. This has been my story, and I, like many others, would love to know yours.

CPSIA information can be obtained
at www.ICGtesting.com
Printed in the USA
LVHW081448230121
677295LV00003B/10